1972

This book may be

FO

fine will be cha

I WAS JUST THINKING—

by Elinor Parker

A BIRTHDAY GARLAND

100 STORY POEMS

MOST GRACIOUS MAJESTY

100 POEMS ABOUT PEOPLE

I WAS JUST THINKING-

A BOOK OF ESSAYS SELECTED BY

Elinor Parker

Wood Engravings by Clare Leighton

Thomas Y. Crowell Company, New York

Grateful acknowledgment is made to the following copyright holders for permission to reprint copyrighted matter in this book:

Constable and Company Limited and Robert Gathorne-Hardy for "The Kaleidoscope" and "Happiness" from *Trivia* by Logan Pearsall Smith.

E. P. Dutton & Co., Inc., for "The Beauty of Shadow" from *Poems and the Spring of Joy* by Mary Webb, copyright 1927 by E. P. Dutton & Co., Inc. (also by permission of Jonathan Cape Limited, London).

Harcourt, Brace and Company for "Things to Write" from *All Trivia* by Logan Pearsall Smith, copyright 1921, 1945 by Harcourt, Brace and Company, Inc.

Harper & Brothers for "Memorandum" from *One Man's Meat* by E. B. White, copyright 1941 by E. B. White.

Houghton Mifflin Company for "Writers and Talkers" from *Ponkapog Papers* by Thomas Bailey Aldrich, copyright 1903 by Thomas Bailey Aldrich.

Alfred A. Knopf, Inc., for "Interlude" from *The National Parks* by Freeman Tilden, copyright 1951 by Alfred A. Knopf, Inc.

J. B. Lippincott Company for "On Visiting Bookshops" from *Essays* by Christopher Morley, copyright 1927, 1954 by Christopher Morley.

Methuen & Co. Ltd. for "The Mowing of a Field" from *Hills and the Sea* by Hilaire Belloc, copyright 1906 by Hilaire Belloc, and "The Town Week" from *Fireside and Sunshine* by E. V. Lucas, copyright 1906 by E. V. Lucas.

A. D. Peters for "My First Article" from *Delight* by J. B. Priestley, copyright 1949 by J. B. Priestley (published by Harper & Brothers and by William Heinemann Limited).

G. P. Putnam's Sons for "April Second" from *An Almanac for Moderns* by Donald Culross Peattie, copyright 1935 by Donald Culross Peattie.

Rinehart & Company, Inc., for "The Headlong Wave" from *The Outermost House* by Henry Beston, copyright 1928, 1949 by Henry Beston.

Sheed and Ward Incorporated and Miss Dorothy Collins for "A Piece of Chalk" from *Tremendous Trifles* by G. K. Chesterton, copyright 1909.

William Sloane Associates, Inc., for "June—Spring Rain" from *The Twelve Seasons* by Joseph Wood Krutch, copyright 1949 by Joseph Wood Krutch.

James Thurber for "There's No Place Like Home," copyright © 1937 The New Yorker Magazine, Inc.

The Viking Press, Inc., for "Dial Tone" from *Under Whatever Sky* by Irwin Edman, copyright 1951 by Irwin Edman.

Mrs. Sheila Wheeler for "The Pleasures of Ignorance" from *The Pleasures of Ignorance* by Robert Lynd, copyright 1921 by Robert Lynd.

The World Publishing Company for "Fadiman's Law of Optimum Improvement" from *Party of One* by Clifton Fadiman, copyright 1955 by Clifton Fadiman.

Yale University Press for "On the Difference Between Wit and Humor" from *Chimney Pot Papers* by Charles S. Brooks, copyright 1919 by Charles S. Brooks.

❋ FOREWORD ❋

THE ESSAY is the most elastic of prose forms—it can be profound, a philosophic search for truth; serious, a piece of literary or artistic criticism; very personal, a reminiscence or an expression of likes and dislikes; detached, recounting the foibles of others; gently humorous or uproariously funny; long—Thoreau's *Walden* is an essay of book length—or short —Smith's *Trivia* are miniature essays complete in two or three paragraphs. An essay can be exactly what its author wants it to be.

The dictionary says an essay is "a literary composition, analytical or interpretive, dealing with its subject from a more or less limited or personal standpoint." David Daiches, who has edited a volume of essays, calls it "the most self-indulgent of literary forms." Clifton Fadiman, an essayist himself, says "the familiar essayist . . . exerts charm, not that he may persuade me to do anything, but solely for the pleasure of it."

In this collection criticism and sermons have been omitted, although nearly every essay included contains a kernel of truth whether the shell surrounding it is hard or soft. We wished to bring together representative authors from the sixteenth century Francis Bacon, the first essayist writing in English, down to the present day when the essay is still flourishing, its most frequent forms being the lightly humorous piece and the thoughtful observation of nature; but while the object was to cover the field historically it was equally important that the essays chosen should meet the qualification of giving pleasure to the reader. There is something for every mood. When fiction strikes the wrong note, biography is unsympathetic, history too serious, the reader can find in essays that satisfaction of being in complete harmony with the author which comes nearest to equaling the pleasures of reading poetry.

Contents

I. READING, WRITING, AND TALKING

II. OUT OF DOORS

III. TRAVELING

IV. THIS AND THAT

I WAS JUST THINKING—

*

* PART I *

READING, WRITING,
AND TALKING

ALEXANDER SMITH

(1830–1867)

On the Writing of Essays

THE ESSAY, as a literary form, resembles the lyric, in so far as it is moulded by some central mood—whimsical, serious, or satirical. Give the mood, and the essay, from the first sentence to the last, grows around it as the cocoon grows around the silkworm. The essay-writer is a chartered libertine, and a law unto himself. A quick ear and eye, an ability to discern the infinite suggestiveness of common things, a brooding meditative spirit, are all that the essayist requires to start business with. Jacques, in "As You Like It," had the makings of a charming essayist. It is not the essayist's duty to inform, to build pathways through metaphysical morasses, to cancel abuses, any more than it is the duty of the poet to do these things. Incidentally he may do something in that way, just as the poet may, but it is not his duty, and should not be expected of him. Skylarks are primarily created to sing, although a whole choir of them may be baked in pies and brought to table; they were born to make music, although they may incidentally stay the pangs of vulgar hunger.

The essayist is a kind of poet in prose, and if questioned

harshly as to his uses, he might be unable to render a better apology for his existence than a flower might. The essay should be pure literature as the poem is pure literature. The essayist wears a lance, but he cares more for the sharpness of its point than for the pennon that flutters on it, than for the banner of the captain under whom he serves. He plays with death as Hamlet plays with Yorick's skull, and he reads the morals—strangely stern, often, for such fragrant lodging—which are folded up in the bosoms of roses. He has no pride, and is deficient in a sense of the congruity and fitness of things. He lifts a pebble from the ground, and puts it aside more carefully than any gem; and on a nail in a cottage-door he will hang the mantle of his thought, heavily brocaded with the gold of rhetoric. He finds his way into the Elysian fields through portals the most shabby and commonplace.

The essayist plays with his subject, now in whimsical, now in grave, now in melancholy mood. He lies upon the idle grassy bank, like Jacques, letting the world flow past him, and from this thing and the other he extracts his mirth and his moralities. His main gift is an eye to discover the suggestiveness of common things; to find a sermon in the most unpromising texts. Beyond the vital hint, the first step, his discourses are not beholden to their titles. Let him take up the most trivial subject, and it will lead him away to the great questions over which the serious imagination loves to brood—fortune, mutability, death—just as inevitably as the runnel, trickling among the summer hills, on which sheep are bleating, leads you to the sea; or as, turning down the first street you come to in the city, you are led finally, albeit by many an intricacy, out into the open country, with its waste places and its woods, where you are lost in a sense of strangeness and solitariness.

The world is to the meditative man what the mulberry plant is to the silkworm. The essay-writer has no lack of subject-matter. He has the day that is passing over his head; and, if unsatisfied with that, he has the world's six thousand years to depasture his gay or serious humour upon. I idle away my time here, and I am finding new subjects every hour. Everything I see or hear is an essay in bud. The world is everywhere whispering essays, and one need only be the world's amanuensis. The proverbial expression which last evening the clown dropped as he trudged homeward to supper, the light of the setting sun on his face, expands before me to a dozen pages. The coffin of the pauper, which to-day I saw carried carelessly along, is as good a subject as the funeral procession of an emperor. Craped drum and banner add nothing to death; penury and disrespect take nothing away. Incontinently my thought moves like a slow-paced hearse with sable nodding plumes.

Two rustic lovers, whispering between the darkening hedges, is as potent to project my mind into the tender passion as if I had seen Romeo touch the cheek of Juliet in the moonlight garden. Seeing a curly-headed child asleep in the sunshine before a cottage-door is sufficient excuse for a discourse on childhood; quite as good as if I had seen infant Cain asleep in the lap of Eve with Adam looking on. A lark cannot rise to heaven without raising as many thoughts as there are notes in its song. Dawn cannot pour its white light on my village without starting from their dim lair a hundred reminiscences; nor can sunset burn above yonder trees in the west without attracting to itself the melancholy of a lifetime. When spring unfolds her green leaves I would be provoked to indite an essay on hope and youth, were it not that it is already writ in the carols of the birds; and I might be tempted in autumn to improve the occasion, were it not for the rustle of the withered leaves as I walk through the woods. Compared with that simple music, the saddest-cadenced words have but a shallow meaning.

The essayist who feeds his thoughts upon the segment of the world which surrounds him cannot avoid being an egotist; but then his egotism is not unpleasing. If he be without taint of boastfulness, of self-sufficiency, of hungry vanity, the world will not press the charge home. If a man discourses continually of his wines, his plate, his titled acquaintances, the number and quality of his horses, his men-servants, he must discourse very skilfully indeed if he escapes being called a coxcomb. If a man speaks of death—tells you that the idea of it continually haunts him, that he has the most insatiable curiosity as to death and dying, that his thought mines in churchyards like a "demon-mole"—no one is specially offended, and that this is a dull fellow is the hardest thing likely to be said of him.

Only, the egotism that overcrows you is offensive, that exalts trifles and takes pleasure in them, that suggests superiority in matters of equipage and furniture; and the egotism is offensive, because it runs counter to and jostles your self-complacency. The egotism which rises no higher than the grave is of a solitary and a hermit kind—it crosses no man's path, it disturbs no man's *amour propre*. You may offend a man if you say you are as rich as he, as wise as he, as handsome as he. You offend no man if you tell him that, like him, you have to die. The king, in his crown and coronation robes, will allow the beggar to claim that relationship with him. To have to die is a distinction of which no man is proud. The speaking about one's self is not necessarily offensive. A modest, truthful man speaks better about himself than about anything else, and on that subject his speech is likely to be most profitable to his hearers. Certainly, there is no subject with which he is better acquainted, and on which he has a better title to be heard. And it is this egotism, this perpetual reference to self, in which the charm of the essayist resides.

If a man is worth knowing at all, he is worth knowing well. The essayist gives you his thoughts, and lets you know, in addition, how he came by them. He has nothing to conceal; he throws open his doors and windows, and lets him enter who will. You like to walk round peculiar or important men as you like to walk round a building, to view it from different points, and in different lights. Of the essayist, when his mood is communicative, you obtain a full picture. You are made his contemporary and familiar friend. You enter into his humours and his seriousness. You are made heir of his whims, prejudices, and playfulness. You walk through the whole nature of him as you walk through the streets of Pompeii, looking into the interior of stately mansions, reading the satirical scribblings on the walls. And the essayist's habit of not only giving you his thoughts, but telling you how he came by them, is interesting, because it shews you by what alchemy the ruder world becomes transmuted into the finer. We like to know the lineage of ideas, just as we like to know the lineage of great earls and swift race horses. We like to know that the discovery of the law of gravitation was born of the fall of an apple in an English garden on a summer afternoon. Essays written after this fashion are racy of the soil in which they grow, as you taste the lava in the vines grown on the slopes of Etna, they say. There is a healthy Gascon flavour in Montaigne's Essays; and Charles Lamb's are scented with the primroses of Covent Garden.

The essayist does not usually appear early in the literary history of a country: he comes naturally after the poet and the chronicler. His habit of mind is leisurely; he does not write from any special stress of passionate impulse; he does not create material so much as he comments upon material already existing. It is essential for him that books should have been written, and that they should, at least to some extent, have been read and digested. He is usually full of allusions and references, and these his reader must be able to follow and understand. And in this literary walk, as in most others, the giants came first; Montaigne and Lord Bacon were our earliest essayists, and, as yet, they are our best. In point of style, these essays are different from anything that

could now be produced. Not only is the thinking different
—the manner of setting forth the thinking is different
also. We despair of reaching the thought, we despair
equally of reaching the language. We can no more bring
back their turns of sentence than we can bring back their
tournaments. Montaigne, in his serious moods, has a curiously rich and intricate eloquence; and Bacon's sentence
bends beneath the weight of his thought, like a branch
beneath the weight of its fruit. Bacon seems to have
written his essays with Shakespeare's pen.

There is a certain want of ease about the old writers
which has an irresistible charm. The language flows like
a stream over a pebbled bed, with propulsion, eddy, and
sweet recoil—the pebbles, if retarding movement, giving
ring and dimple to the surface, and breaking the whole
into babbling music. There is a ceremoniousness in the
mental habits of these ancients. Their intellectual garniture is picturesque, like the garniture of their bodies.
Their thoughts are courtly and high mannered. A sin-
gular analogy exists between the personal attire of a
period and its written style. The peaked beard, the
starched collar, the quilted doublet, have their corres-
pondences in the high sentence and elaborate ornament
(worked upon the thought like figures upon tapestry)
of Sidney and Spenser. In Pope's day men wore rapiers,
and their weapons they carried with them into literature,
and frequently unsheathed them too. They knew how to
stab to the heart with an epigram. Style went out with
the men who wore knee-breeches and buckles in their
shoes. We write more easily now; but in our easy writing

there is ever a taint of flippancy: our writing is to theirs, what shooting-coat and wideawake are to doublet and plumed hat.

* * *

And on style depends the success of the essayist. Montaigne said the most familiar things in the finest way. Goldsmith could not be termed a thinker; but everything he touched he brightened, as after a month of dry weather, the shower brightens the dusty shrubbery of a suburban villa. The world is not so much in need of new thoughts as that when thought grows old and worn with usage it should, like current coin, be called in, and, from the mint of genius, reissued fresh and new. Love is an old story enough, but in every generation it is reborn, in the downcast eyes and blushes of young maidens. And so, although he fluttered in Eden, Cupid is young today. If Montaigne had lived in Dreamthorp, as I am now living, had he written essays as I am now writing them, his English Essays would have been as good as his Gascon ones. Looking on, the country cart would not for nothing have passed him on the road to market, the setting sun would be arrested in its splendid colours, the idle chimes of the church would be translated into a thoughtful music. As it is, the village life goes on, and there is no result. My sentences are not much more brilliant than the speeches of the clowns; in my book there is little more life than there is in the market-place on the days when there is no market.

FRANCIS BACON

(1561–1626)

Of Studies

STUDIES serve for delight, for ornament, and for ability. Their chief use for delight, is in privateness and retiring; for ornament, is in discourse; and for ability, is in the judgement and disposition of business; for expert men can execute, and perhaps judge of particulars, one by one: but the general counsels, and the plots and marshalling of affairs come best from those that are learned.

To spend too much time in studies, is sloth; to use them too much for ornament, is affectation; to make judgement wholly by their rules, is the humour of a scholar: they perfect nature, and are perfected by experience: for natural abilities are like natural plants, that need pruning by study; and studies themselves do give forth directions too much at large, except they be bounded in by experience. Crafty men contemn studies, simple men admire them, and wise men use them; for they teach not their own use; but that is a wisdom without them and above them, won by observation. Read not to contradict and confute, nor to believe and take for granted, nor to find talk and discourse, but to weigh and consider.

Some books are to be tasted, others to be swallowed, and some few to be chewed and digested; that is, some books are to be read only in parts; others to be read but not curiously; and some few to be read wholly, and with diligence and attention. Some books also may be read by deputy, and extracts made of them by others; but that would be only in the less important arguments and the meaner sort of books; else distilled books are, like common distilled waters, flashy things.

Reading maketh a full man; conference a ready man; and writing an exact man; and, therefore, if a man write little, he had need have a great memory; if he confer little, he had need have a present wit; and if he read little, he had need have much cunning, to seem to know that he doth not. Histories make men wise; poets, witty; the mathematics, subtle; natural philosophy, deep; moral, grave; logic and rhetoric, able to contend: *Abeunt studia in mores;* nay, there is no stand or impediment in the wit, but may be wrought out by fit studies: like as diseases of the body may have appropriate exercises; bowling is good for the stone and reins, shooting for the lungs and breast, gentle walking for the stomach, riding for the head and the like; so if a man's wit be wandering, let him study the mathematics; for in demonstrations, if his wit be called away never so little, he must begin again; if his wit be not apt to distinguish or find difference, let him study the schoolmen; for they are *Cymini sectores*. If he be not apt to beat over matters, and to call up one thing to prove and illustrate another, let him study the lawyers' cases: so every defect of the mind may have a special receipt.

WASHINGTON IRVING

(1783–1859)

The Art of Book-Making

> If that severe doom of Synesius be true,—
> "It is a greater offence to steal dead men's
> labor, than their clothes," what shall become
> of most writers?
>
> BURTON's *Anatomy of Melancholy*

I HAVE often wondered at the extreme fecundity of
the press, and how it comes to pass that so many heads,
on which nature seemed to have inflicted the curse of
barrenness, should teem with voluminous productions.
As a man travels on, however, in the journey of life, his
objects of wonder daily diminish, and he is continually
finding out some very simple cause for some great matter
of marvel. Thus have I chanced, in my peregrinations
about this great metropolis, to blunder upon a scene
which unfolded to me some of the mysteries of the
book-making craft, and at once put an end to my
astonishment.

I was one summer's day loitering through the great
saloons of the British Museum, with that listlessness with
which one is apt to saunter about a museum in warm
weather; sometimes lolling over the glass cases of miner-

als, sometimes studying the hieroglyphics on an Egyptian
mummy, and sometimes trying, with nearly equal success, to comprehend the allegorical paintings of the lofty
ceilings. Whilst I was gazing about in this idle way, my
attention was attracted to a distant door at the end of a
suite of apartments. It was closed, but every now and then
it would open, and some strange-favored being, generally clothed in black, would steal forth, and glide
through the rooms, without noticing any of the surrounding objects. There was an air of mystery about
this that piqued my languid curiosity, and I determined
to attempt the passage of that strait, and to explore the
unknown regions beyond. The door yielded to my hand,
with that facility with which the portals of enchanted
castles yield to the adventurous knight-errant.

I found myself in a spacious chamber, surrounded
with great cases of venerable books. Above the cases,
and just under the cornice, were arranged a great number
of black-looking portraits of ancient authors. About the
room were placed long tables, with stands for reading
and writing, at which sat many pale, studious personages,
poring intently over dusty volumes, rummaging among
mouldy manuscripts, and taking copious notes of their
contents. A hushed stillness reigned through this mysterious apartment, excepting that you might hear the racing
of pens over sheets of paper, or occasionally the deep
sigh of one of these sages, as he shifted his position to
turn over the page of an old folio; doubtless arising from
that hollowness and flatulency incident to learned re-
search.

Now and then one of these personages would write

something on a small slip of paper, and ring a bell, where-
upon a familiar would appear, take the paper in profound
silence, glide out of the room, and return shortly loaded
with ponderous tomes, upon which the other would fall
tooth and nail with famished voracity. I had no longer a
doubt that I had happened upon a body of magi, deeply
engaged in the study of occult sciences. The scene reminded me of an old Arabian tale, of a philosopher shut
up in an enchanted library, in the bosom of a mountain,
which opened only once a year; where he made the
spirits of the place bring him books of all kinds of dark
knowledge, so that at the end of the year, when the magic
portal once more swung open on its hinges, he issued
forth so versed in forbidden lore, as to be able to soar
above the heads of the multitude, and to control the
powers of nature.

My curiosity being now fully aroused, I whispered to
one of the familiars, as he was about to leave the room,
and begged an interpretation of the strange scene before
me. A few words were sufficient for the purpose. I found
that these mysterious personages, whom I had mistaken
for magi, were principally authors, and in the very act
of manufacturing books. I was, in fact, in the reading-
room of the great British Library—an immense collection
of volumes of all ages and languages, many of which are
now forgotten, and most of which are seldom read: one
of these sequestered pools of obsolete literature, to which
modern authors repair, and draw buckets full of classic
lore, or "pure English, undefiled," wherewith to swell
their own scanty rills of thought.

Being now in possession of the secret, I sat down in a

corner, and watched the process of this book-manufactory. I noticed one lean, bilious-looking wight, who sought none but the most worm-eaten volumes, printed in black-letter. He was evidently constructing some work of profound erudition, that would be purchased by every man who wished to be thought learned, placed upon a conspicuous shelf of his library, or laid open upon his table; but never read. I observed him, now and then, draw a large fragment of biscuit out of his pocket, and gnaw; whether it was his dinner, or whether he was endeavoring to keep off that exhaustion of the stomach produced by much pondering over dry works, I leave to harder students than myself to determine.

There was one dapper little gentleman in bright-colored clothes, with a chirping, gossiping expression of countenance, who had all the appearance of an author on good terms with his bookseller. After considering him attentively, I recognized in him a diligent getter-up of miscellaneous works, which bustled off well with the trade. I was curious to see how he manufactured his wares. He made more stir and show of business than any of the others; dipping into various books, fluttering over the leaves of manuscripts, taking a morsel out of one, a morsel out of another, "line upon line, precept upon precept, here a little and there a little." The contents of his book seemed to be as heterogeneous as those of the witches' caldron in Macbeth. It was here a finger and there a thumb, toe of frog and blind-worm's sting, with his own gossip poured in like "baboon's blood," to make the medley "slab and good."

After all, thought I, may not this pilfering disposition be implanted in authors for wise purposes; may it not be the way in which Providence has taken care that the seeds of knowledge and wisdom shall be preserved from age to age, in spite of the inevitable decay of the works in which they were first produced? We see that nature has wisely, though whimsically, provided for the conveyance of seeds from clime to clime, in the maws of certain birds; so that animals, which, in themselves, are little better than carrion, and apparently in the lawless plunderers of the orchard and cornfield, are, in fact, nature's carriers to disperse and perpetuate her blessings. In like manner, the beauties and fine thoughts of ancient and obsolete authors are caught up by these flights of predatory writers, and cast forth again to flourish and bear fruit in a remote and distant tract of time. Many of their works, also, undergo a kind of metempsychosis, and spring up under new forms. What was formerly a ponderous history, revives in the shape of a romance— an old legend changes into a modern play—and a sober philosophical treatise furnishes the body for a whole series of bouncing and sparkling essays. Thus it is in the clearing of our American woodlands: where we burn down a forest of stately pines, a progeny of dwarf oaks start up in their place; and we never see the prostrate trunk of a tree mouldering into soil, but it gives birth to a whole tribe of fungi.

Let us not, then, lament over the decay and oblivion into which ancient writers descend; they do but submit to the great law of nature, which declares that all

sublunary shapes of matter shall be limited in their dur-
ation, but which decrees, also, that their elements shall
never perish. Generation after generation, both in animal
and vegetable life, passes away, but the vital principle is
transmitted to posterity, and the species continue to flourish. Thus, also, do authors beget authors, and having produced a numerous progeny, in a good old age they sleep
with their fathers, that is to say, with the authors who
preceded them—and from whom they had stolen.

Whilst I was indulging in these rambling fancies, I had
leaned my head against a pile of reverend folios. Whether
it was owing to the soporific emanations from these
works; or to the profound quiet of the room; or to the
lassitude arising from much wandering; or to an unlucky
habit of napping at improper times and places, with which
I am grievously afflicted, so it was, that I fell into a doze.
Still, however, my imagination continued busy, and indeed the same scene remained before my mind's eye,
only a little changed in some of the details. I dreamt
that the chamber was still decorated with the portraits
of ancient authors, but that the number was increased.
The long tables had disappeared, and, in place of the
sage magi, I beheld a ragged, threadbare throng, such as
may be seen plying about the great repository of cast-off
clothes, Monmouth Street. Whenever they seized upon a
book, by one of those incongruities common to dreams,
methought it turned into a garment of foreign or antique
fashion, with which they proceeded to equip themselves.
I noticed, however, that no one pretended to clothe
himself from any particular suit, but took a sleeve from

one, a cape from another, a skirt from a third, thus decking himself out piecemeal, while some of his original rags would peep out from among his borrowed finery.

There was a portly, rosy, well-fed parson, whom I observed ogling several mouldy polemical writers through an eye-glass. He soon contrived to slip on the voluminous mantle of one of the old fathers, and, having purloined the gray beard of another, endeavored to look exceedingly wise; but the smirking commonplace of his countenance set at naught all the trappings of wisdom. One sickly-looking gentleman was busied embroidering a very flimsy garment with gold thread drawn out of several old court-dresses of the reign of Queen Elizabeth. Another had trimmed himself magnificently from an illuminated manuscript, had stuck a nosegay in his bosom, culled from "The Paradise of Daintie Devices," and having put Sir Philip Sidney's hat on one side of his head, strutted off with an exquisite air of vulgar elegance. A third, who was but of puny dimensions, had bolstered himself out bravely with the spoils from several obscure tracts of philosophy, so that he had a very imposing front; but he was lamentably tattered in rear, and I perceived that he had patched his small-clothes with scraps of parchment from a Latin author.

There were some well-dressed gentlemen, it is true, who only helped themselves to a gem or so, which sparkled among their own ornaments, without eclipsing them. Some, too, seemed to contemplate the costumes of the old writers, merely to imbibe their principles of taste, and to catch their air and spirit; but I grieve to say, that too many were apt to array themselves from top to toe in the patchwork manner I have mentioned. I shall not omit to speak of one genius, in drab breeches and gaiters, and an Arcadian hat, who had a violent propensity to the pastoral, but whose rural wanderings had been confined to the classic haunts of Primrose Hill, and the solitudes of the Regent's Park. He had decked himself in wreaths and ribbons from all the old pastoral poets, and, hanging his head on one side, went about with a fantastical, lackadaisical air, "babbling about green fields." But the personage that most struck my attention was a pragmatical old gentleman, in clerical robes, with a remarkably large and square, but bald head. He entered the room wheezing and puffing, elbowed his way through the throng, with a look of sturdy self-confidence, and having laid hands upon a thick Greek quarto, clapped it upon his head, and swept majestically away in a formidable frizzled wig.

In the height of this literary masquerade, a cry suddenly resounded from every side, of "Thieves! thieves!" I looked, and lo! the portraits about the wall became animated! The old authors thrust out, first a head, then a shoulder, from the canvas, looked down curiously, for an instant, upon the motley throng, and then descended with fury in their eyes, to claim their rifled property. The scene of scampering and hubbub that ensued baffles all description. The unhappy culprits endeavored in vain to escape with their plunder. On one side might be seen half a dozen old monks stripping a modern professor; on another, there was sad devastation carried into the ranks of modern dramatic writers. Beaumont and Fletcher, side by side, raged round the field like Castor and Pollux, and sturdy Ben Jonson enacted more wonders than when a volunteer with the army in Flanders. As to the dapper little compiler of farragos, mentioned some time since, he had arrayed himself in as many patches and colors as Harlequin, and there was as fierce a contention of claimants about him as about the dead body of Patroclus. I was grieved to see many men, to whom I had been accustomed to look upon with awe and reverence, fain to steal off with scarce a rag to cover their nakedness. Just then my eye was caught by the pragmatical old gentleman in the Greek grizzled wig, who was scrambling away in sore affright with half a score of authors in full cry after him! They were close upon his haunches: in a twinkling off went his wig; at every turn some strip of raiment was peeled away; until in a few moments, from his domineering pomp, he shrunk into a little, pursy, "chopped bald shot," and made his exit with only a few tags and rags fluttering at his back.

There was something so ludicrous in the catastrophe of this learned Theban, that I burst into an immoderate fit of laughter, which broke the whole illusion. The tumult and the scuffle were at an end. The chamber resumed its usual appearance. The old authors shrunk back into their picture-frames, and hung in shadowy solemnity along the walls. In short, I found myself wide awake in my corner, with the whole assemblage of bookworms gazing at me with astonishment. Nothing of the dream had been real but my burst of laughter, a sound never before heard in that grave sanctuary, and so abhorrent to the ears of wisdom as to electrify the fraternity.

The librarian now stepped up to me, and demanded whether I had a card of admission. At first I did not comprehend him, but I soon found that the library was a kind of literary "preserve," subject to game-laws, and that no one must presume to hunt there without special license and permission. In a word, I stood convicted of being an arrant poacher, and was glad to make a precipitate retreat, lest I should have a whole pack of authors let loose upon me.

CHARLES LAMB

(1775–1834)

Detached Thoughts on Books and Reading

> To mind the inside of a book is to entertain
> one's self with the forced product of another
> man's brain. Now I think a man of quality
> and breeding may be much amused with the
> natural sprouts of his own.
>
> LORD FOPPINGTON IN *The Relapse*

AN INGENIOUS acquaintance of my own was so much struck with this bright sally of his Lordship, that he has left off reading altogether, to the great improvement of his originality. At the hazard of losing some credit on this head, I must confess that I dedicate no inconsiderable portion of my time to other people's thoughts. I dream away my life in others' speculations. I love to lose myself in other men's minds. When I am not walking, I am reading; I cannot sit and think. Books think for me.

I have no repugnances. Shaftesbury is not too genteel for me, nor Jonathan Wild too low. I can read any thing which I call a *book*. There are things in that shape which I cannot allow for such.

In this catalogue of *books which are not books—biblia a-biblia*—I reckon Court Calendars, Directories, Pocket

Books, Draught Boards bound and lettered at the back, Scientific Treatises, Almanacks, Statutes at Large; the works of Hume, Gibbon, Robertson, Beattie, Soame Jenyns, and, generally, all those volumes which "no gentleman's library should be without": the Histories of Flavius Josephus (that learned Jew), and Paley's Moral Philosophy. With these exceptions, I can read almost any thing. I bless my stars for a taste so catholic, so unexcluding.

I confess that it moves my spleen to see these *things in books' clothing* perched upon shelves, like false saints, usurpers of true shrines, intruders into the sanctuary, thrusting out the legitimate occupants. To reach down a well-bound semblance of a volume, and hope it some kind-hearted play-book, then, opening what "seem its leaves," to come bolt upon a withering Population Essay. To expect a Steele, or a Farquhar, and find—Adam Smith. To view a well-arranged assortment of blackheaded encyclopaedias (Anglicanas or Metropolitanas) set out in an array of Russia, or Morocco, when a tithe of that good leather would comfortably re-clothe my shivering folios; would renovate Paracelsus himself, and enable old Raymond Lully to look like himself again in the world. I never see these imposters, but I long to strip them, to warm my ragged veterans in their spoils.

To be strong-backed and neat-bound is the desideratum of a volume. Magnificence comes after. This, when it can be afforded, is not to be lavished upon all kinds of books indiscriminately. I would not dress a set of Magazines, for instance, in full suit. The dishabille, or half-binding (with Russia backs ever) is *our* costume. A Shakspeare, or a Milton (unless the first editions), it were mere foppery to trick out in gay apparel. The possession of them confers no distinction. The exterior of them (the things themselves being so common), strange to say, raises no sweet emotions, no tickling sense of property in the owner. Thomson's Seasons, again, looks best (I maintain it) a little torn, and dog's-eared. How beautiful to a genuine lover of reading are the sullied leaves, and worn out appearance, nay, the very odour (beyond Russia), if we would not forget kind feelings in fastidiousness, of an old "Circulating Library" Tom Jones, or Vicar of Wakefield! How they speak of the thousand thumbs, that have turned over their pages with delight! —of the lone sempstress, whom they may have cheered (milliner, or harder-working mantua-maker) after her long day's needle-toil, running far into midnight, when she has snatched an hour, ill-spared from sleep, to steep her cares, as in some Lethean cup, in spelling out their enchanting contents! Who would have them a whit less soiled? What better condition could we desire to see them in?

In some respects the better a book is, the less it demands from binding. Fielding, Smollett, Sterne, and all that class of perpetually self-reproductive volumes—Great Nature's Stereotypes—we see them individually perish with less regret, because we know the copies of them to be "eterne." But where a book is at once both good and rare—where the individual is almost the species, and when *that* perishes,

We know not where is that Promethean torch
That can its light relumine—

such a book, for instance, as the Life of the Duke of
Newcastle, by his Duchess—no casket is rich enough, no
casing sufficiently durable, to honour and keep safe such
a jewel.

Not only rare volumes of this description, which seem
hopeless ever to be reprinted; but old editions of writers,
such as Sir Philip Sydney, Bishop Taylor, Milton in his
prose-works, Fuller—of whom we *have* reprints, yet the
books themselves though they go about, and are talked
of here and there, we know, have not endenizened themselves (nor possibly ever will) in the national heart, so
as to become stock books—it is good to possess these in
durable and costly covers. I do not care for a First Folio
of Shakspeare. I rather prefer the common editions of
Rowe and Tonson, without notes, and with *plates*, which,
being so execrably bad, serve as maps, or modest remem-
brancers, to the text; and without pretending to any
supposable emulation with it, are so much better than the
Shakspeare gallery *engravings*, which *did*. I have a com-
munity of feeling with my countrymen about his Plays,
and I like those editions of him best, which have been
oftenest tumbled about and handled.—On the contrary,
I cannot read Beaumont and Fletcher but in Folio. The
Octavo editions are painful to look at. I have no sympathy
with them. If they were as much read as the current
editions of the other poet, I should prefer them in that
shape to the older one. I do not know a more heartless
sight than the reprint of the Anatomy of Melancholy.
What need was there of unearthing the bones of that

fantastic old great man, to expose them in a winding-sheet of the newest fashion to modern censure? what hapless stationer could dream of Burton ever becoming popular?—The Wretched Malone could not do worse, when he bribed the sexton of Stratford church to let him white-wash the painted effigy of old Shakspeare, which stood there, in rude but lively fashion depicted, to the very colour of the cheek, the eye, the eye-brow, hair, the very dress he used to wear—the only authentic testimony we had, however imperfect, of these curious parts and parcels of him. They covered him over with a coat of white paint. By —— ——, if I had been a justice of peace for Warwickshire, I would have clapt both commentator and sexton fast in the stocks, for a pair of meddling sacrilegious varlets.

I think I see them at their work—these sapient trouble-tombs.

Shall I be thought fantastical, if I confess, that the names of some of our poets sound sweeter, and have a finer relish to the ear—to mine, at least—than that of Milton or of Shakspeare? It may be, that the latter are more staled and rung upon in common discourse. The sweetest names, and which carry a perfume in the mention, are, Kit Marlowe, Drayton, Drummond of Haw-thornden, and Cowley.

Much depends upon *when* and *where* you read a book. In the five or six impatient minutes, before the dinner is quite ready, who would think of taking up the Fairy Queen for a stop-gap, or a volume of Bishop Andrewes' sermons?

Milton almost requires a solemn service of music to

be played before you enter upon him. But he brings his music, to which, who listens, had need bring docile thoughts, and purged ears.

Winter evenings—the world shut out—with less of ceremony the gentle Shakspeare enters. At such a season, the Tempest, or his own Winter's Tale—

These two poets you cannot avoid reading aloud—to yourself, or (as it chances) to some single person listening. More than one—and it degenerates into an audience.

Books of quick interest, that hurry on for incidents, are for the eye to glide over only. It will not do to read them out. I could never listen to even the better kind of modern novels without extreme irksomeness.

A newspaper, read out, is intolerable. In some of the Bank offices it is the custom (to save so much individual time) for one of the clerks—who is the best scholar—to commence upon the Times or the Chronicle, and recite its entire contents aloud *pro bono publico*. With every advantage of lungs and elocution, the effect is singularly vapid. In barbers' shops and public-houses a fellow will get up, and spell out a paragraph which he communicates as some discovery. Another follows with *his* selection. So the entire journal transpires at length by piece-meal. Seldom-readers are slow readers, and without this expedient no one in the company would probably ever travel through the contents of a whole paper.

Newspapers always excite curiosity. No one ever lays one down without a feeling of disappointment.

What an eternal time that gentleman in black, at

Nando's, keeps the paper! I am sick of hearing the waiter bawling out incessantly, "the Chronicle is in hand, Sir."

Coming in to an inn at night—having ordered your supper—what can be more delightful than to find lying in the window-seat, left there time out of mind by the carelessness of some former guest—two or three numbers of the old Town and Country Magazine, with its amusing tête-à-tête pictures—"The Royal Lover and Lady G——;" "The Melting Platonic and the Old Beau," —and such like antiquated scandal? Would you exchange it—at that time, and in that place—for a better book?

Poor Tobin, who latterly fell blind, did not regret it so much for the weightier kinds of reading—the Paradise Lost, or Comus, he could have *read* to him—but he missed the pleasure of skimming over with his own eye a magazine, or a light pamphlet.

I should not care to be caught in the serious avenues of some cathedral alone, and reading *Candide*.

I do not remember a more whimsical surprise than having been once detected—by a familiar damsel—reclined at my ease upon the grass, on Primrose Hill (her Cythera), reading—*Pamela*. There was nothing in the book to make a man seriously ashamed at the exposure; but as she seated herself down by me, and seemed determined to read in company, I could have wished it had been—any other book. We read on very sociably for a few pages; and, not finding the author much to her taste, she got up, and—went away. Gentle casuist, I leave it to thee to conjecture, whether the blush (for there was one between us) was the property of the nymph or the swain in this dilemma. From me you shall never get the secret.

I am not much a friend to out-of-doors reading. I cannot settle my spirits to it. I knew a Unitarian minister, who was generally to be seen upon Snow-hill (as yet Skinner's street *was not*), between the hours of ten and eleven in the morning, studying a volume of Lardner. I owe this to have been a strain of abstraction beyond my reach. I used to admire how he sidled along, keeping clear of secular contacts. An illiterate encounter with a porter's knot, or a bread basket, would have quickly put to flight all the theology I am master of, and have left me worse than indifferent to the five points.

There is a class of street-readers, whom I can never contemplate without affection—the poor gentry, who, not having wherewithal to buy or hire a book, filch a little learning at the open stalls—the owner, with his hard eye, casting envious looks at them all the while, and thinking when they will have done. Venturing tenderly, page after page, expecting every moment when he shall interpose his interdict, and yet unable to deny themselves the gratification, they "snatch a fearful joy." Martin B—, in this way, by daily fragments, got through two volumes of Clarissa, when the stallkeeper damped his laudable ambition, by asking him (it was his younger days) whether he meant to purchase the work. M. declares, that under no circumstance in his life did he ever peruse a book with half the satisfaction which he took in those uneasy snatches. A quaint poetess of our day has moralised upon this subject in two very touching but homely stanzas.

I saw a boy with eager eye
Open a book upon a stall,
And read, as he'd devour it all;
Which when the stall-man did espy,
Soon to the boy I heard him call,
"You, Sir, you never buy a book,
Therefore in one you shall not look."
The boy pass'd slowly on, and with a sigh
He wish'd he never had been taught to read,
Then of the old churl's books he should have had no need.

Of sufferings the poor have many,
Which never can the rich annoy:
I soon perceiv'd another boy,
Who look'd as if he'd not had any
Food, for that day at least—enjoy
The sight of cold meat in a tavern larder.
This boy's case, then thought I, is surely harder,
Thus hungry, longing, thus without a penny,
Beholding choice of dainty-dressed meat:
No wonder if he wish he ne'er had learn'd to eat.

THOMAS BAILEY ALDRICH

(1836–1907)

Writers and Talkers

As a class, literary men do not shine in conversation. The scintillating and playful essayist whom you pictured to yourself as the most genial and entertaining of companions, turns out to be a shy and untalkable individual, who chills you with his reticence when you chance to meet him. The poet whose fascinating volume you always drop into your gripsack on your summer vacation—the poet whom you have so long desired to know personally —is a moody and abstracted middle-aged gentleman, who fails to catch your name on introduction, and seems the avatar of the commonplace. The witty and ferocious critic whom your fancy had painted as a literary cannibal with a morbid appetite for tender young poets—the writer of those caustic and scholarly reviews which you never neglect to read—destroys the un-lifelike portrait you had drawn by appearing before you as a personage of slender limb and deprecating glance, who stammers and makes a painful spectacle of himself when you ask him his opinion of "The Glees of the Gulches," by Popocatepetl Jones. The slender, dark-haired novelist of your imagination, with epigrammatic points to his mustache, suddenly takes the shape of a short, smoothly-shaven blond man, whose conversation does not sparkle at all, and you were on the lookout for the most brilliant of verbal fireworks.

Perhaps it is a dramatist you have idealized. Fresh from witnessing his delightful comedy of manners, you meet him face to face only to discover that his own manners are anything but delightful. The play and the playwright are two very distinct entities. You grow skeptical touching the truth of Buffon's assertion that the style is the man himself. Who that has encountered his favorite author in the flesh has not sometimes been a little, if not wholly, disappointed?

After all, is it not expecting too much to expect a novelist to talk as cleverly as the clever characters in his novels? Must a dramatist necessarily go about armed to the teeth with crisp dialogue? May not a poet be allowed to lay aside his singing-robes and put on a conventional dress-suit when he dines out? Why is it not permissible in him to be as prosaic and tiresome as the rest of the company? He usually is.

CHARLES S. BROOKS

(1878–1934)

On the Difference Between Wit and Humor

I AM not sure that I can draw an exact line between wit and humor. Perhaps the distinction is so subtle that only those persons can decide who have long white beards. But even an ignorant man, so long as he is clear of Bedlam, may have an opinion.

I am quite positive that of the two, humor is the more comfortable and more livable quality. Humorous persons, if their gift is genuine and not a mere shine upon the surface, are always agreeable companions and they sit through the evening best. They have pleasant mouths turned up at the corners. To these corners the great Master of marionettes has fixed the strings and he holds them in his nimblest fingers to twitch them at the slightest jest. But the mouth of a merely witty man is hard and sour until the moment of its discharge. Nor is the flash from a witty man always comforting, whereas a humorous man radiates a general pleasure and is like another candle in the room.

I admire wit, but I have no real liking for it. It has

been too often employed against me, whereas humor is always an ally. It never points an impertinent finger into my defects. Humorous persons do not sit like explosives on a fuse. They are safe and easy comrades. But a wit's tongue is as sharp as a donkey's stick. I may gallop the faster for its prodding, yet the touch behind is too persuasive for any comfort.

I sat lately at dinner with a notoriously witty person (a really witty man) whom our hostess had introduced to provide the entertainment. I had read many of his reviews of books and plays, and while I confess their wit and brilliancy, I had thought them to be hard and intellectual and lacking in all that broader base of humor which aims at truth. His writing—catching the bad habit of the time —is too ready to proclaim a paradox and to assert the unusual, to throw aside in contempt the valuable haystack in a fine search for a paltry needle. His reviews are seldom right—as most of us see the right—but they sparkle and hold one's interest for their perversity and unexpected turns.

In conversation I found him much as I had found him in his writing—although, strictly speaking, it was not a conversation, which requires an interchange of word and idea and is turn about. A conversation should not be a market where one sells and another buys. Rather, it should be a bargaining back and forth, and each person should be both merchant and buyer. My rubber plant for your victrola, each offering what he has and seeking his deficiency. It was my friend B——— who fairly put the case when he said that he liked so much to talk that he was willing to pay for his audience by listening in his turn.

But this was a speech and a lecture. He loosed on us from the cold spigot of his intellect a steady flow of literary allusion—a practice which he professes to hold in scorn—and wit and epigram. He seemed torn from the pages of Meredith. He talked like ink. I had believed before that only people in books could talk as he did, and then only when their author had blotted and scratched their performance for a seventh time before he sent it to the printer. To me it was an entirely new experience, for my usual acquaintances are good common honest daytime woollen folk and they seldom average better than one bright thing in an evening.

Now I would not seek that kind of man as a companion with whom to be becalmed in a sailboat, and I would not wish to go to the country with him, least of all to the North Woods or any place outside of civilization. I am sure that he would sulk if he were deprived of an audience. He would be crotchety at breakfast across his bacon. Certainly for the woods a humorous man is better company, for his humor in mischance comforts both him and you. A humorous man—and here lies the heart of the matter—a humorous man has the high gift of regarding an annoyance in the very stroke of it as another man shall regard it when the annoyance is long past. If a humorous person falls out of a canoe he knows the exquisite jest while his head is still bobbing in the cold water. A witty man, on the contrary, is sour until he is changed and dry: but in a week's time when company is about, he will make a comic story of it.

My friend A——— with whom I went once into the Canadian woods has genuine humor, and no one can be a more satisfactory comrade. I do not recall that he said many comic things, and at bottom he was serious as the best humorists are. But in him there was a kind of joy and exaltation that lasted throughout the day. If the duffle were piled too high and fell about his ears, if the dinner was burned or the tent blew down in a driving storm at night, he met these mishaps as though they were the very things he had come north to get, as though without them the trip would have lacked its spice. This is an easy philosophy in retrospect but hard when the wet canvas falls across you and the rain beats in. A——— laughed at the very moment of disaster as another man will laugh later in an easy chair. I see him now swinging his axe for firewood to dry ourselves when we were spilled in a rapids; and again, while pitching our tent on a sandy beach when another storm had drowned us. And there is a certain cry of his (dully, *Wow!* on paper) expressive to the initiated of all things gay, which could never issue from the mouth of a merely witty man.

Real humor is primarily human—or divine, to be exact —and after that the fun may follow naturally in its order. Not long ago I saw Louis Jouvet of the French Company play Sir Andrew Aguecheek. It was a most humorous performance of the part, and the reason is that the actor made no primary effort to be funny. It was the humanity of his playing, making his audience love him first of all, that provoked the comedy. His long thin legs were comical and so was his drawling talk, but the very heart and essence was this love he started in his audience. Poor fellow! how delightfully he smoothed the feathers in his hat! How he feared to fight the duel! It was easy to love such a dear silly human fellow. A merely witty player might have drawn as many laughs, but there would not have been the catching at the heart.

As for books and the wit or humor of their pages, it appears that wit fades, whereas humor lasts. Humor uses permanent nutgalls. But is there anything more melancholy than the wit of another generation? In the first place, this wit is intertwined with forgotten circumstance. It hangs on a fashion—on the style of a coat. It arose from a forgotten bit of gossip. In the play of words the sources of the pun are lost. It is like a local jest in a narrow coterie, barren to an outsider. Sydney Smith was the most celebrated wit of his day, but he is dull reading now. Blackwood's at its first issue was a witty daring sheet, but for us the pages are stagnant. I suppose that no one now laughs at the witticisms of Thomas Hood. Where are the wits of yesteryear? Yet the humor of Falstaff and Lamb and Fielding remains and is a reminder to us that humor, to be real, must be founded on humanity and on truth.

LOGAN PEARSALL SMITH

(1865–1946)

Things to Write

WHAT things there are to write, if one could only write them! My mind is full of gleaming thoughts; gay moods and mysterious, mothlike meditations hover in my imagination, fanning their painted wings. They would make my fortune if I could catch them; but always the rarest, those freaked with azure and the deepest crimson, flutter away beyond my reach.

The ever-baffled chase of these filmy nothings often seems, for one of sober years in a sad world, a trifling occupation. But have I not read of the great Kings of Persia who used to ride out to hawk for butterflies, nor deemed this pastime beneath their royal dignity?

J. B. PRIESTLEY

(1894-   )

My First Article

WHEN I was sixteen I was already writing articles and offering them to any kind of editor whose address I could discover. These articles were of two kinds. The first, which I signed portentously "J. Boynton Priestley," were serious, very serious, indeed, and were full of words like "renaissance" and "significance" and "aftermath," and suggested that their author was about a hundred and fifty years old. And nobody wanted them. They could not be given away. No editor had a body of readers old enough for such articles. The other kind were skits and burlesques and general funny work, written from the grimly determined humourous standpoint of the school magazine. One of these was accepted, printed and paid for by a London humourous weekly. I had arrived. (And my father, not to be found wanting on such an occasion, presented me with one of his fourpenny cigars, with which, as I fancy he guessed, I had been secretly experimenting for some months.) The issue of the weekly containing my article burst upon the world. Riding inside a tram from Duckworth Lane to Godwin Street, Bradford,

I saw a middle-aged woman opening this very copy of the weekly, little knowing, as I made haste to tell myself, that one of its group of brilliant contributors was not two yards away. I watched her turn the pages. She came to *the* page; she hesitated; she stopped, she began to read my article. Ah—what delight! But mine, of course, not hers. And not mine for long, not more than a second, for then there settled on her face an expression I have noticed ten thousand times since, and have for years now tried not to notice—the typical expression of the reader, the audience, the customer, the patron. How shall I describe this curious look? There is in it a kind of innocence—and otherwise I think I would have stopped writing years ago—but mixed a trifle sourly with this admirable innocence is a flavouring of wariness, perhaps a touch of suspicion itself. "Well, what have we here?" it enquires dubiously. And then the proud and smirking Poet and Maker falls ten thousand feet into dubiety. So ever since that tram ride I have never caught a glimpse of the reader, the audience, the customer, the patron, without instantly trying to wedge myself into the rocks above the black tarn of doubt. As I do this, there is the flash of a blue wing—and the bird of delight has flown.

CHRISTOPHER MORLEY

(1890–1957)

On Visiting Bookshops

IT IS a curious thing that so many people only go into a bookshop when they happen to need some particular book. Do they never drop in for a little innocent carouse and refreshment? There are some knightly souls who even go so far as to make their visits to bookshops a kind of chivalrous errantry at large. They go in not because they need any certain volume, but because they feel that there may be some book that needs them. Some wistful, little forgotten sheaf of loveliness, long pining away on an upper shelf—why not ride up, fling her across your charger (or your charge account), and gallop away. Be a little knightly, you booklovers!

The lack of intelligence with which people use book-shops is, one supposes, no more flagrant than the lack of intelligence with which we use all the rest of the machinery of civilization. In this age, and particularly in this city, we haven't time to be intelligent.

A queer thing about books, if you open your heart to them, is the instant and irresistible way they follow you with their appeal. You know at once, if you are clairvoyant in these matters (librevoyant, one might say), when you have met your book. You may dally and evade, you may go on about your affairs, but the paragraph of prose your eye fell upon, or the snatch of verses, or perhaps only the spirit and flavour of the volume, more divined than reasonably noted, will follow you. A few lines glimpsed on a page may alter your whole trend of thought for the day, reverse the currents of the mind, change the profile of the city. The other evening, in a subway car, we were reading Walter de la Mare's interesting little essay about Rupert Brooke. His discussion of children, their dreaming ways, their exalted simplicity and absorption, changed the whole tenor of our voyage by some magical chemistry of thought. It was no longer a wild, barbaric struggle with our fellowmen, but a venture of faith and recompense, taking us home to the bedtime of a child.

The moment when one meets a book and knows, beyond shadow of doubt, that that book must be his—not necessarily now, but some time—is among the happiest excitements of the spirit. An indescribable virtue effuses from some books. One can feel the radiations of an honest book long before one sees it, if one has a sensitive pulse for such affairs. Its honour and truth will speak through the advertising. Its mind and heart will cry out even underneath the extravagance of jacket-blurbings. Some shrewd soul, who understands books, remarked some time ago on the editorial page of the *Sun's* book review that no superlative on a jacket had ever done the book an atom of good. He was right, as far as the true bookster is concerned. We choose our dinner not by the wrappers, but by the veining and gristle of the meat within.

The other day, prowling about a bookshop, we came upon two paper-bound copies of a little book of poems by Alice Meynell. They had been there for at least two years. We had seen them before, a year or more ago, but had not looked into them fearing to be tempted. This time we ventured. We came upon two poems—"To O, Of Her Dark Eyes," and "A Wind of Clear Weather in England." The book was ours—or rather, we were its, though we did not yield at once. We came back the next day and got it. We are still wondering how a book like that could stay in the shop so long. Once we had it, the day was different. The sky was sluiced with a clearer blue, air and sunlight blended for a keener intake of the lungs, faces seen along the street moved us with a livelier shock of interest and surprise. The wind that moved over Sussex and blew Mrs. Meynell's heart into her lines was still flowing across the ribs and ledges of our distant scene.

There is no mistaking a real book when one meets it. It is like falling in love, and like that colossal adventure it is an experience of great social import. Even as the tranced swain, the booklover yearns to tell others of his bliss. He writes letters about it, adds it to the postscript of all manner of communications, intrudes it into telephone messages, and insists on his friends writing down the title of the find. Like the simple-hearted betrothed, once certain of his conquest, "I want you to love her, too!" It is a jealous passion also. He feels a little indignant if he finds that any one else has discovered the book, too. He sees an enthusiastic review—very likely in the *New Republic*—and says, with great scorn, "I read the book three months ago." There are even some perversions of passion by which a booklover loses much of his affection for his pet if he sees it too highly commended by some rival critic.

This sharp ecstasy of discovering books for one's self is not always widespread. There are many who, for one reason or another, prefer to have their books found out for them. But for the complete zealot nothing transcends the zest of pioneering for himself. And therefore working for a publisher is, to a certain type of mind, a never-failing fascination. As H. M. Tomlinson says in *Old Junk*, that fascinating collection of sensitive and beautifully poised sketches which came to us recently with a shock of thrilling delight:

> *To come upon a craft rigged so, though at her moorings, and with sails furled, her slender poles upspringing from the bright plane of a brimming harbour, is to me as rare and sensational a delight as the rediscovery, when idling with a book, of a favourite lyric.*

To read just that passage, and the phrase *the bright plane of a brimming harbour*, is one of those "rare and sensational delights" that set the mind moving on lovely journeys of its own, and mark off visits to a bookshop not as casual errands of reason, but as necessary acts of devotion. We visit bookshops not so often to buy any one special book, but rather to rediscover, in the happier and more expressive words of others, our own encumbered soul.

IRWIN EDMAN

(1896–1954)

Dial Tone

"WAIT until you hear the dial tone," the telephone company admonishes, "or you will not be able to make your connection." Sometimes the dial tone is heard at once, and there is a pleasure in the recognition, a sense that all is well. I have long cherished the belief that in reading one has a similar exerience. In the first page, sometimes in the first paragraph, of a writer whom one has never read before, one is aware, in the tone and cadence of the sentences themselves, that one has the dial tone, or, perhaps, that the connection has been made. There will doubtless be a good deal about the book that will be a disappointment: perhaps the tone will be lost or the connection broken. But what a thrill it is to come upon it, if for the moment only.

I am prepared to accept all manner of explanation of the phenomenon. Obviously it is often dependent on the state of well-being of the reader. Given a high enough euphoria in the reader, and the Congressional Record or a report of the Department of Agriculture could give such a note. But I have learned seldom to distrust a first impression. Something about the movement, the melody, the rhythm of the sentences tells me within half a minute that I am in the presence of authentic writing, not manufactured or faked, but the unmistakable life-blood of literature.

✳ PART II ✳

OUT OF DOORS

HENRY D. THOREAU

(1817–1862)

Where I Lived, and What I Lived For

At a certain season of our life we are accustomed to consider every spot as the possible site of a house. I have thus surveyed the country on every side within a dozen miles of where I live. In imagination I have bought all the farms in succession, for all were to be bought, and I knew their price. I walked over each farmer's premises, tasted his wild apples, discoursed on husbandry with him, took his farm at his price, at any price, mortgaging it to him in my mind; even put a higher price on it,—took everything but a deed on it,—took his word for his deed, for I dearly love to talk,—cultivated it, and him too to some extent, I trust, and withdrew when I have enjoyed it long enough, leaving him to carry it on. This experience entitled me to be regarded as a sort of real-estate broker by my friends. Wherever I sat, there I might live, and the landscape radiated from me accordingly. What is a house but a *sedes*, a seat?—better if a country seat.

I discovered many a site for a house not likely to be soon improved, which some might have thought too far from the village, but to my eyes the village was too far from it. Well, there I might live, I said; and there I did live, for an hour, a summer and a winter life, saw how I could let the years run off, buffet the winter through, and see the spring come in. The future inhabitants of this region, wherever they may place their houses, may be sure that they have been anticipated. An afternoon sufficed to lay out the land into orchard, woodlot, and pasture, and to decide what fine oaks or pines should be left to stand before the door, and whence each blasted tree could be seen to the best advantage; and then I let it lie, fallow perchance, for a man is rich in proportion to the number of things which he can afford to let alone.

My imagination carried me so far that I even had the refusal of several farms,—the refusal was all I wanted,— but I never got my fingers burned by actual possession. The nearest that I came to actual possession was when I bought the Hollowell place, and had begun to sort my seeds, and collected materials with which to make a wheelbarrow to carry it on or off with; but before the owner gave me a deed of it, his wife—every man has such a wife—changed her mind and wished to keep it, and he offered me ten dollars to release him. Now, to speak the truth, I had but ten cents in the world, and it surpassed my arithmetic to tell, if I was that man who had ten cents, or who had a farm, or ten dollars, or all together. However, I let him keep the ten dollars and the farm too, for I had carried it far enough; or rather, to be generous, I sold him the farm for just what I gave for it, and, as he was not a rich man, made him a present of ten dollars, and still had my ten cents, and seeds, and materials for a wheelbarrow left. I found thus that I had been a rich man without any damage to my property. But I retained the landscape, and I have since annually carried off what it yielded without a wheelbarrow. With respect to land-scapes,—

> *I am monarch of all I* survey,
> *My right there is none to dispute.*

I have frequently seen a poet withdraw, having en-joyed the most valuable part of a farm, while the crusty farmer supposed that he had got a few wild apples only. Why, the owner does not know it for many years when a poet has put his farm in rhyme, the most admirable kind of invisible fence, has fairly impounded it, milked it, skimmed it, and got all the cream, and left the farmer only the skimmed milk.

The real attractions of the Hollowell farm, to me, were: its complete retirement, being about two miles from the village, half a mile from the nearest neighbor, and sep-arated from the highway by a broad field; its bounding on the river, which the owner said protected it by its fogs from frosts in the spring, though that was nothing to me; the gray color and ruinous state of the house and barn, and the dilapidated fences, which put such an interval between me and the last occupant; the hollow and lichen-covered apple trees, gnawed by rabbits, showing what kind of neighbors I should have; but above all, the rec-ollection I had of it from my earliest voyages up the river when the house was concealed behind a dense grove of red maples, through which I heard the house-dog bark.

I was in haste to buy it, before the proprietor finished getting out some rocks, cutting down the hollow apple trees, and grubbing up some young birches which had sprung up in the pasture, or, in short, had made any more of his improvements. To enjoy these advantages I was ready to carry it on; like Atlas, to take the work on my shoulders,—I never heard what compensation he received for that,—and do all those things which had no other motive or excuse but that I might pay for it and be unmolested in my possession of it; for I knew all the while that it would yield the most abundant crop of the kind I wanted if I could only afford to let it alone. But it turned out as I have said.

All that I could say, then, with respect to farming on a large scale (I have always cultivated a garden), was that I had had my seeds ready. Many think that seeds improve with age. I have no doubt that time discriminates between the good and the bad: and when at last I shall plant, I shall be less likely to be disappointed. But I would say to my fellows, once for all, As long as possible live free and uncommitted. It makes but little difference whether you are committed to a farm or the county jail.

Old Cato, whose "De Re Rusticâ" is my "cultivator," says, and the only translation I have seen makes sheer nonsense of the passage, "When you think of getting a farm, turn it thus in your mind, not to buy greedily; nor spare your pains to look at it, and do not think it enough to go round it once. The oftener you go there the more it will please you, if it is good." I think I shall not buy greedily, but go round and round it as long as I live, and be buried in it first, that it may please me the more at last.

The present was my next experiment of this kind, which I purpose to describe more at length; for convenience, putting the experience of two years into one. As I have said, I do not propose to write an ode to dejection, but to brag as lustily as chanticleer in the morning, standing on his roost, if only to wake my neighbors up.

When first I took up my abode in the woods, that is, began to spend my nights as well as days there, which, by accident, was on Independence Day, or the fourth of July, 1845, my house was not finished for winter, but was merely a defence against the rain, without plastering or chimney, the walls being of rough weatherstained boards, with wide chinks, which made it cool at night. The upright white hewn studs and freshly planed door and window casings gave it a clean and airy look, especially in the morning, when its timbers were saturated with dew, so that I fancied that by noon some sweet gum would exude from them. To my imagination it retained throughout the day more or less of this auroral character, reminding me of a certain house on a mountain which I have visited the year before. This was an airy and unplastered cabin, fit to entertain a travelling god, and where a goddess might trail her garments. The winds which passed over my dwelling were such as sweep over the ridges of mountains, bearing the broken strains, or celestial parts only, of terrestrial music. The morning wind forever blows, the poem of creation is uninterrupted; but few are the ears that hear it. Olympus is but the outside of the earth everywhere.

The only house I had been the owner of before, if I except a boat, was a tent, which I used occasionally when making excursions in the summer, and this is still rolled up in my garret; but the boat, after passing from hand to hand, has gone down the stream of time. With this more substantial shelter about me, I had made some progress toward settling in the world. This frame, so slightly clad, was a sort of crystallization around me, and reacted on the builder. It was suggestive somewhat as a picture in outlines. I did not need to go out doors to take the air, for the atmosphere within had lost none of its freshness. It was not so much within doors as behind a door where I sat, even in the rainiest weather. The Harivansa says, "An abode without birds is like a meat without seasoning." Such was not my abode, for I found myself suddenly neighbor to the birds; not by having imprisoned one, but having caged myself near them. I was not only nearer to some of those which commonly frequent the garden and the orchard, but to those wilder and more thrilling songsters of the forest which never, or rarely, serenade a villager,—the wood thrush, the veery, the scarlet tanager, the field sparrow, the whippoorwill, and many others.

I was seated by the shore of a small pond, about a mile and a half south of the village of Concord and somewhat higher than it, in the midst of an extensive wood between that town and Lincoln, and about two miles south of that our only field known to fame, Concord Battle Ground; but I was so low in the woods that the opposite shore, half a mile off, like the rest, covered with wood,

was my most distant horizon. For the first week, wherever I looked out on the pond it impressed me like a
tarn high up on the side of a mountain, its bottom far
above the surface of other lakes, and, as the sun arose, I
saw it throwing off its mighty clothing of mist, and here
and there, by degrees, its soft ripples or its smooth re-
flecting surface were revealed, while the mists, like ghosts,
were stealthily withdrawing in every direction into the
woods, as at the breaking up of some nocturnal conventicle.
The very dew seemed to hang upon the trees later into
the day than usual, as on the sides of mountains.

This small lake was of most value as a neighbor in the
intervals of a gentle rain storm in August, when, both air
and water being perfectly still, but the sky overcast, mid-
afternoon had all the serenity of evening, and the wood
thrush sang around, and was heard from shore to shore.
A lake like this is never smoother than at such a time;
and the clear portion of the air above it being shallow and
darkened by clouds, the water, full of light, and reflections, becomes a lower heaven itself so much the more
important. From a hill top near by, where the wood had
recently been cut off, there was a pleasing vista southward
across the pond, through a wide indentation in the hills
which form the shore there, where their opposite sides
sloping toward each other suggested a stream flowing out
in that direction through a wooded valley, but stream
there was none. That way I looked between and over the
near green hills to some distant and higher ones in the
horizon, tinged with blue. Indeed, by standing on tiptoe
I could catch a glimpse of some of the peaks of the still

bluer and more distant mountain ranges in the northwest, those true-blue coins from heaven's own mint, and also of some portion of the village. But in other directions, even from this point, I could not see over or beyond the woods which surrounded me.

It is well to have some water in your neighborhood, to give buoyancy to and float the earth. One value even of the smallest well is that when you look into it you see that the earth is not continent but insular. This is as important as that it keeps butter cool. When I looked across the pond from the peak toward the Sudbury meadows, which in time of flood I distinguished elevated perhaps by a mirage in their seething valley, like a coin in a basin, all the earth beyond the pond appeared like a thin crust insulated and floated even by this small sheet of intervening water, and I was reminded that this on which I dwelt was but *dry land*.

Though the view from my door was still more contracted, I did not feel crowded or confined in the least. There was pasture enough for my imagination. The low shrub-oak plateau to which the opposite shore arose, stretched away toward the prairies of the West and the steppes of Tartary, affording ample room for all the roving families of men. "There are none happy in the world but beings who enjoy freely a vast horizon,"— said Damodara, when his herds required new and larger pastures.

Both place and time were changed and I dwelt nearer to those parts of the universe and to those eras in history which had most attracted me. Where I live was as far off as many a region viewed nightly by astronomers. We are wont to imagine rare and delectable places in some remote and more celestial corner of the system, behind the constellation of Cassiopeia's Chair, far from noise and disturbance. I discovered that my house actually had its site in such a withdrawn, but forever new and unprofaned, part of the universe. If it were worth the while to settle in those parts near to the Pleiades or the Hyades, to Aldebaran or Altair, then I was really there, or at an equal remoteness from the life which I had left behind, dwindled and twinkling with as fine a ray to my nearest neighbor, and to be seen only in moonless nights by him. Such was that part of creation where I had squatted:

> *There was a shepherd that did live,*
> *And held his thoughts as high*
> *As were the mounts whereon his flocks*
> *Did hourly feed him by.*

What should we think of the shepherd's life if his flocks always wandered to higher pastures than his thoughts?

Every morning was a cheerful invitation to make my life of equal simplicity, and I may say innocence, with Nature herself. I have been as sincere a worshipper of Aurora as the Greeks. I got up early and bathed in the pond; that was a religious exercise, and one of the best things which I did. They say that characters were engraven on the bathing tub of king Tching-thang to this effect: "Renew thyself completely each day; do it again, and again, and forever again." I can understand that. Morning brings back the heroic ages. I was as much affected by the faint hum of a mosquito making its invisible and unimaginable tour through my apartment at earliest dawn, when I was sitting with door and windows open, as I could be by any trumpet that ever sang of fame. It was Homer's requiem; itself an Iliad and Odyssey in the air, singing its own wrath and wanderings. There was something cosmical about it; a standing advertisement, till forbidden, of the everlasting vigor and fertility of the world. The morning, which is the most memorable season of the day, is the awakening hour. Then there is least somnolence in us; and for an hour, at least, some part of us awakes which slumbers all the rest of the day and night.

Little is to be expected of that day, if it can be called a day, to which we are not awakened by our Genius, but by the mechanical nudgings of some servitor, are not awakened by our own newly acquired force and aspirations from within, accompanied by the undulations of celestial music, instead of factory bells, and a fragrance filling the air—to a higher life than we fell asleep from; and thus the darkness bear its fruit, and prove itself to be good, no less than the light. That man who does not believe that each day contains an earlier, more sacred, and auroral hour than he has yet profaned, has despaired of life, and is pursuing a descending and darkening way. After a partial cessation of his sensuous life, the soul of man, or its organs rather, are reinvigorated each day, and his Genius tries again what noble life it can make.

All memorable events, I should say, transpire in morning time and in a morning atmosphere. The Vedas say, "All intelligences awake with the morning." Poetry and art, and the fairest and most memorable of the actions of men, date from such an hour. All poets and heroes, like Memnon, are the children of Aurora, and emit their music at sunrise. To him whose elastic and vigorous thoughts keep pace with the sun, the day is a perpetual morning. It matters not what the clocks say or the attitudes and labors of men. Morning is when I am awake and there is a dawn in me. Moral reform is the effort to throw off sleep. Why is it that men give so poor an account of their day if they have not been slumbering? They are not such poor calculators. If they had not been overcome with drowsiness they would have performed something. The millions are awake enough for physical labor; but only one in a million is awake enough for effective intellectual exertion, only one in a hundred millions to a poetic or divine life. To be awake is to be alive. I have never yet met a man who was quite awake. How could I have looked him in the face?

We must learn to reawaken and keep ourselves awake, not by mechanical aids, but by an infinite expectation of the dawn, which does not forsake us in our soundest sleep. I know of no more encouraging fact than the unquestionable ability of man to elevate his life by a conscious endeavor. It is something to be able to paint a particular picture, or to carve a statue, and so to make a few objects beautiful; but it is far more glorious to carve and paint the very atmosphere and medium through which we look, which morally we can do. To effect the quality of the day, that is the highest of arts. Every man is tasked to make his life, even in its details, worthy of the contemplation of his most elevated and critical hour. If we refused, or rather used up, such paltry information as we get, the oracles would distinctly inform us how this might be done.

I went to the woods because I wished to live deliberately, to front only the essential facts of life, and see if I could not learn what it had to teach, and not, when I came to die, discover that I had not lived. I did not wish to live what was not life, living is so dear; nor did I wish to practise resignation, unless it was quite necessary. I wanted to live deep and suck out all the marrow of life, to live so sturdily and Spartan-like as to put to rout all that was not life, to cut a broad swath and shave close, to drive life into a corner, and reduce it to its lowest terms, and, if it proved to be mean, why then to get the whole and genuine meanness of it, and publish its meanness to the world; or if it were sublime, to know it by experience, and be able to give a true account of it in my next excursion. For most men, it appears to me, are in a strange uncertainty about it, whether it is of the devil or of God, and have *somewhat hastily* concluded that it is the chief end of man here to "glorify God and enjoy him forever."

Still we live meanly, like ants; though the fable tells us that we were long ago changed into men; like pygmies we fight with cranes; it is error upon error, and clout upon clout, and our best virtue has for its occasion a superfluous and evitable wretchedness. Our life is frittered away by detail. An honest man has hardly need to count more than his ten fingers, or in extreme cases he may add his ten toes, and lump the rest. Simplicity, simplicity, simplicity! I say, let your affairs be as two or three, and not a hundred or a thousand; instead of a million count half a dozen, and keep your accounts on your thumb nail. In the midst of this chopping sea of civilized life, such are the clouds and storms and quicksands and thousand-and-one items to be allowed for, that a man has to live, if he would not founder and go to the bottom and not make his port at all, by dead reckoning, and he must be a great calculator indeed who succeeds. Simplify, simplify. Instead of three meals a day, if it be necessary eat but one; instead of a hundred dishes, five; and reduce other things in proportion.

*   *   *

Let us spend one day as deliberately as Nature, and not be thrown off the track by every nutshell and mosquito's wing that falls on the rails. Let us rise early and fast, or break fast, gently and without perturbation; let company come and let company go, let the bells ring and the children cry,—determined to make a day of it. Why should we knock under and go with the stream? Let us not be upset and overwhelmed in that terrible rapid and whirlpool called a dinner, situated in the meridian shallows. Weather this danger and you are safe, for the rest of the way is down hill. With unrelaxed nerves, with morning vigor, sail by it, looking another way, tied to the mast like Ulysses. If the engine whistles, let it whistle till it is hoarse for its pains. If the bell rings, why should we run? We will consider what kind of music they are like. Let us settle ourselves, and work and wedge our feet downward through the mud and slush of opinion and prejudice, and tradition, and delusion and appearance, that alluvion which covers the globe, through Paris and London, through New York and Boston and Concord, through church and state, through poetry and philosophy and religion, till we come to a hard bottom and rocks in place, which we can call *reality*, and say, This is, and no mistake; and then begin, having a *point d'appui*, below freshet and frost and fire, a place where you might found a wall or a state, or set a lamp-post safely, or perhaps a gauge, not a Nilometer, but a Realometer, that future ages might know how deep a freshet of shams and appearances had gathered from time to time. If you stand right fronting and face to face to a fact, you will see the sun glimmer on both its surfaces, as if it were a scimitar, and feel its sweet edge dividing you through the heart and marrow, and so you will happily conclude your mortal career. Be it life or death, we crave only reality. If we are really dying, let us hear the rattle in our throats and feel cold in the extremities; if we are alive, let us go about our business.

Time is but the stream I go a-fishing in. I drink at it; but while I drink I see the sandy bottom and detect how shallow it is. Its thin current slides away, but eternity remains. I would drink deeper; fish in the sky, whose bottom is pebbly with stars. I cannot count one. I know not the first letter of the alphabet, I have always been regretting that I was not as wise as the day I was born. The intellect is a cleaver; it discerns and rifts its way into the secret of things. I do not wish to be any more busy with my hands than is necessary. My head is hands and feet. I feel all my best faculties concentrated in it. My instinct tells me that my head is an organ for burrowing, as some creatures use their snout and forepaws, and with it I would mine and burrow my way through these hills. I think that the richest vein is somewhere hereabouts; so by the divining rod and thin rising vapors I judge; and here I will begin to mine.

HILAIRE BELLOC

(1870–1953)

The Mowing of a Field

THERE is a valley in South England remote from ambition and from fear, where the passage of strangers is rare and unperceived, and where the scent of the grass in summer is breathed only by those who are native to that unvisited land. The roads to the Channel do not traverse it; they choose upon either side easier passes over the range. One track alone leads up through it to the hills, and this is changeable: now green where men have little occasion to go, now a good road where it nears the homesteads and the barns. The woods grow steep above the slopes; they reach sometimes the very summit of the heights, or, when they cannot attain them, fill in and clothe the combes. And, in between, along the floor of the valley, deep pastures and their silence are bordered by lawns of chalky grass and the small yew trees of the Downs.

The clouds that visit its sky reveal themselves beyond the one great rise, and sail, white and enormous, to the other, and sink beyond that other. But the plains above which they have travelled and the Weald to which they go, the people of the valley cannot see and hardly recall. The wind, when it reaches such fields, is no longer a gale from the salt, but fruitful and soft, an inland breeze; and those whose blood was nourished here feel in that wind the fruitfulness of our orchards and all the life that all things draw from the air.

In this place, when I was a boy, I pushed through a fringe of beeches that made a complete screen between me and the world, and I came to a glade called No Man's Land. I climbed beyond it, and I was surprised and glad, because from the ridge of that glade I saw the sea. To this place very lately I returned.

The many things that I recovered as I came up the countryside were not less charming than when a distant memory had enshrined them, but much more. Whatever veil is thrown by a longing recollection had not intensified nor even made more mysterious the beauty of that happy ground; not in my very dreams of morning had I, in exile, seen it more beloved or more rare. Much also that I had forgotten now returned to me as I approached —a group of elms, a little turn of the parson's wall, a small paddock beyond the graveyard close, cherished by one man, with a low wall of very old stone guarding it all around. And all these things fulfilled and amplified my delight, till even the good vision of the place, which I had kept so many years, left me and was replaced by its better reality. "Here," I said to myself, "is a symbol of what some say is reserved for the soul: pleasure of a kind which cannot be imagined save in the moment when at last it is attained."

When I came to my own gate and my own field, and had before me the house I knew, I looked around a little (though it was already evening), and I saw that the grass was standing as it should stand when it is ready for the scythe. For in this, as in everything that a man can do—of those things at least which are very old—there is an exact moment when they are done best. And it has been remarked of whatever rules us that it works blunderingly, seeing that the good things given to man are not given at the precise moment when they would have filled him with delight. But, whether this be true or false, we can choose the just turn of the seasons in everything we do of our own will, and especially in the making of hay.

Many think that hay is best made when the grass is thickest; and so they delay until it is rank and in flower, and has already heavily pulled the ground. And there is another false reason for delay, which is wet weather. For very few will understand (though it comes year after year) that we have rain always in South England between sickle and the scythe, or say just after the weeks of east wind are over. First we have a week of sudden warmth, as though the South had come to see us all; then we have the weeks of east and south-east wind; and then we have more or less of that rain of which I spoke, and which always astonishes the world. Now it is just before, or during, or at the very end of that rain—but not later—that grass should be cut for hay. True, upland grass, which is always thin, should be cut earlier than the grass in the bottoms and along the water meadows; but not even the latest, even in the wettest seasons, should be left (as it is) to flower and even to seed. For what we get when we store our grass is not a harvest of something ripe, but a thing just caught in its prime before maturity: as witness that our corn and straw are best yellow, but our hay is best green. So also Death should be represented with a scythe and Time with a sickle; for Time can take only what is ripe, but Death comes always too soon.

In a word, then, it is always much easier to cut grass too late than too early; and I, under that evening and come back to these pleasant fields, looked at the grass and knew that it was time. June was in full advance: it was the beginning of that season when the night has already lost her foothold of the earth and hovers over it, never quite descending, but mixing sunset with the dawn.

Next morning, before it was yet broad day, I awoke, and thought of the mowing. The birds were already chattering in the trees beside my window, all except the nightingale, which had left and flown away to the Weald, where he sings all summer by day as well as by night in the oaks and the hazel spinneys, and especially along the little river Adur, one of the rivers of the Weald. The birds and the thought of the mowing had awakened me, and I went down the stairs and along the stone floors to where I could find a scythe; and when I took it from its nail, I remembered how, fourteen years ago, I had last gone out with my scythe, just so, into the fields at morning. In between that day and this were many things, cities and armies, and a confusion of books, mountains and the desert, and horrible great breadths of sea.

When I got out into the long grass the sun was not yet risen, but there were already many colours in the eastern sky, and I made haste to sharpen my scythe, so that I might get to the cutting before the dew should dry. Some say that it is best to wait till all the dew has risen, so as to get the grass quite dry from the very first. But, though it is an advantage to get the grass quite dry, yet it is not worth while to wait till the dew has risen. For, in the first place, you lose many hours of work (and those the coolest), and next—which is more important—you lose that great ease and thickness in cutting which comes of the dew. So I at once began to sharpen my scythe.

There is an art also in the sharpening of a scythe, and it is worth describing carefully. Your blade must be dry, and that is why you will see men rubbing the scythe-blade with grass before they whet it. Then also your rubber must be quite dry, and on this account it is a good thing to lay it on your coat and keep it there during all your day's mowing. The scythe you stand upright, with the blade pointing away from you, and you put your left hand firmly on the back of the blade, grasping it: then you pass the rubber first down one side of the blade-edge and then down the other, beginning near the handle and going on to the point and working quickly and hard. When you first do this you will, perhaps, cut your hand; but it is only at first that such an accident will happen to you.

To tell when the scythe is sharp enough this is the rule. First the stone clangs and grinds against the iron harshly; then it rings musically to one note; then, at last, it purrs

as though the iron and stone were exactly suited. When
you hear this, your scythe is sharp enough; and I, when
I heard it in that June dawn, with everything quite silent
except the birds, let down the scythe and bent myself
to mow.

When one does anything anew, after so many years,
one fears very much for one's trick or habit. But all
things once learnt are easily recoverable, and I very soon
recovered the swing and power of the mower. Mowing
well and mowing badly—or rather not mowing at all—
are separated by very little; as is also true of writing
verse, of playing the fiddle, and of dozens of other things
but of nothing more than of believing. For the bad or
young or untaught mower without tradition, the mower
Promethean, the mower original and contemptuous of
the past, does all these things: He leaves great crescents of
grass uncut. He digs the point of the scythe hard into
the ground with a jerk. He loosens the handles and even
the fastening of the blade. He twists the blade with his
blunders, he blunts the blade, he chips it, dulls it, or breaks
it clean off at the tip. If any one is standing by he cuts
him in the ankle. He sweeps up into the air wildly, with
nothing to resist his stroke. He drags up earth with the
grass, which is like making the meadow bleed. But the
good mower who does things just as they should be done
and have been for a hundred thousand years, falls into
none of these fooleries. He goes forward very steadily,
his scythe-blade just barely missing the ground, every
grass falling; the swish and rhythm of his mowing are
always the same.

So great an art can only be learnt by continual practice; but this much is worth writing down, that, as in all good work, to know the thing with which you work is the core of the affair. Good verse is best written on good paper with an easy pen, not with a lump of coal on a whitewashed wall. The pen thinks for you; and so does the scythe mow for you if you treat it honourably and in a manner that makes it recognize its service. The manner is this. You must regard the scythe as a pendulum that swings, not as a knife that cuts. A good mower puts no more strength into his stroke than into his lifting. Again, stand up to your work. The bad mower, eager and full of pain, leans forward and tries to force the scythe through the grass. The good mower, serene and able, stands as nearly straight as the shape of the scythe will let him, and follows up every stroke closely, moving his left foot forward. Then also let every stroke get well away. Mowing is a thing of ample gestures, like drawing a cartoon. Then, again, get yourself into a mechanical and repetitive mood: be thinking of anything at all but your mowing, and be anxious only when there seems some interruption to the monotony of the sound. In this mowing should be like one's prayers—all of a sort and always the same, and so made that you can establish a monotony and work them, as it were, with half your mind: that happier half, the half that does not bother.

In this way, when I had recovered the art after so many years, I went forward over the field, cutting lane after lane through the grass, and bringing out its most secret essences with the sweep of the scythe until the air was full of odours. At the end of every lane I sharpened my scythe and looked back at the work done, and then carried my scythe down again upon my shoulder to begin another. So, long before the bell rang in the chapel above me—that is, long before six o'clock, which is the time for the *Angelus*—I had many swathes already lying in order parallel like soldiery; and the high grass yet standing, making a great contrast with the shaven part, looked dense and high. As it says in the *Ballad of Val-ès-Dunes*, where—

> *The tall son of the Seven Winds*
> *Came riding out of Hither-hythe,*

and his horse hoofs (you will remember) trampled into the press and made a gap in it, and his sword (as you know)

> *. . . was like a scythe*
> *In Arcus when the grass is high*
> *And all the swathes in order lie,*
> *And there's the bailiff standing by*
> *A-gathering of the tithe.*

So I mowed all that morning, till the houses awoke in the valley, and from some of them rose a little fragrant smoke, and men began to be seen.

I stood still and rested on my scythe to watch the awakening of the village, when I saw coming up to my field a man whom I had known in older times, before I had left the Valley.

He was of that dark silent race upon which all the learned quarrel, but which, by whatever meaningless name

it may be called—Iberian, or Celtic, or what you will—
is the permanent root of all England, and makes England
wealthy and preserves it everywhere, except perhaps in
the Fens and in a part of Yorkshire. Everywhere else
you will find it active and strong. These people are
intensive; their thoughts and their labours turn inward.
It is on account of their presence in these islands that
our gardens are the richest in the world. They also love
low rooms and ample fires and great warm slopes of
thatch. They have, as I believe, an older acquaintance
with the English air than any other of all the strains that
make up England. They hunted in the Weald with stones,
and camped in the pines of the green-sand. They lurked
under the oaks of the upper rivers, and saw the legion-
aries go up, up the straight paved road from the sea. They
helped the few pirates to destroy the towns, and mixed
with those pirates and shared the spoils of the Roman
villas, and were glad to see the captains and the priests
destroyed. They remain; and no admixture of the Frisian
pirates, or the Breton, or the Angevin and Norman con-
querors, has very much affected their cunning eyes.

To this race, I say, belonged the man who now approached me. And he said to me, "Mowing?" And I
answered, "Ar." Then he also said "Ar," as in duty
bound; for so we speak to each other in the Stenes of
the Downs.

Next he told me that, as he had nothing to do, he
would lend me a hand; and I thanked him warmly, or, as
we say, "kindly." For it is a good custom of ours always
to treat bargaining as though it were a courteous pastime;

and though what he was after was money, and what I wanted was his labour at the least pay, yet we both played the comedy that we were free men, the one granting a grace and the other accepting it. For the dry bones of commerce, avarice and method and need, are odious to the Valley; and we cover them up with a pretty body of fiction and observances. Thus, when it comes to buying pigs, the buyer does not begin to decry the pig and the vendor to praise it, as is the custom with lesser men; but tradition makes them do business in this fashion:—

First the buyer will go up to the seller when he sees him in his own steading, and, looking at the pig with admiration, the buyer will say that rain may or may not fall, or that we shall have snow or thunder, according to the time of the year. Then the seller, looking critically at the pig, will agree that the weather is as his friend maintains. There is no haste at all; great leisure marks the dignity of their exchange. And the next step is, that the buyer says: "That's a fine pig you have there, Mr.—" (giving the seller's name). "Ar, powerful fine pig." Then the seller, saying also "Mr." (for twin brothers rocked in one cradle give each other ceremonious observance here), the seller, I say, admits, as though with reluctance, the strength and beauty of the pig, and falls into deep thought. Then the buyer says, as though moved by a great desire, that he is ready to give so much for the pig, naming half the proper price, or a little less. Then the seller remains in silence for some moments; and at last begins to shake his head slowly, till he says: "I don't be thinking of selling the pig, anyways." He will also add that a party only

Wednesday offered him so much for the pig—and he names about double the proper price. Thus all ritual is duly accomplished; and the solemn act is entered upon with reverence and in a spirit of truth. For when the buyer uses this phrase: "I'll tell you what I *will* do," and offers within half a crown of the pig's value, the seller replies that he can refuse him nothing, and names half a crown above its value; the difference is split, the pig is sold, and in the quiet soul of each runs the peace of something accomplished.

Thus do we buy a pig or land or labourer or malt or lime, always with elaboration and set forms; and many a London man has paid double and more for his violence and his greedy haste and very unchivalrous higgling. As happened with the land at Underwaltham, which the mortgagees had begged and implored the estate to take at twelve hundred, and had privately offered to all the world at a thousand, but which a sharp direct man, of the kind that makes great fortunes, a man in a motor-car, a man in a fur coat, a man of few words, bought for two thousand three hundred before my very eyes, protesting that they might take his offer or leave it; and all because he did not begin by praising the land.

Well then, this man I spoke of offered to help me, and he went to get his scythe. But I went into the house and brought out a gallon jar of small ale for him and for me; for the sun was now very warm, and small ale goes well with mowing. When we had drunk some of this ale in mugs called "I see you," we took each a swathe, he a little behind me because he was the better mower; and so for many hours we swung, one before the other, mowing and mowing at the tall grass of the field. And the sun rose to noon and we were still at our mowing; and we ate food, but only for a little while, and we took again to our mowing. And at last there was nothing left but a small square of grass, standing like a square of linesmen who keep their formation, tall and unbroken, with all the dead lying around them when a battle is over and done.

Then for some little time I rested after all those hours; and the man and I talked together, and a long way off we heard in another field the musical sharpening of a scythe.

The sunlight slanted powdered and mellow over the breadth of the valley; for day was nearing its end. I went to fetch rakes from the steading; and when I had come back the last of the grass had fallen, and all the field lay flat and smooth, with the very green short grass in lanes between the dead and yellow swathes.

These swathes we raked into cocks to keep them from the dew against our return at daybreak; and we made the cocks as tall and steep as we could, for in that shape they best keep off the dew, and it is easier also to spread them after the sun has risen. Then we raked up every straggling blade, till the whole field was a clean floor for the tedding and the carrying of the hay next morning. The grass we had mown was but a little over two acres; for that is all the pasture on my little tiny farm.

When we had done all this, there fell upon us the beneficent and deliberate evening; so that as we sat a little while together near the rakes, we saw the valley more solemn and dim around us, and all the trees and hedgerows quite still, and held by a complete silence. Then I paid my companion his wage, and bade him a good night, till we should meet in the same place before sunrise.

He went off with a slow and steady progress, as all our peasants do, making their walking a part of the easy but continual labour of their lives. But I sat on, watching the light creep around towards the north and change, and the waning moon coming up as though by stealth behind the woods of No Man's Land.

G. K. CHESTERTON

(1874–1936)

A Piece of Chalk

I REMEMBER one splendid morning, all blue and silver, in the summer holidays, when I reluctantly tore myself away from the task of doing nothing in particular, and put on a hat of some sort and picked up a walking-stick, and put six very bright-coloured chalks in my pocket. I then went into the kitchen (which, along with the rest of the house, belonged to a very square and sensible old woman in a Sussex village), and asked the owner and occupant of the kitchen if she had any brown paper. She had a great deal; in fact, she had too much; and she mistook the purpose and the rationale of the existence of brown paper. She seemed to have an idea that if a person wanted brown paper he must be wanting to tie up parcels; which was the last thing I wanted to do; indeed, it is a thing which I have found to be beyond my mental capacity. Hence she dwelt very much on the varying qualities of toughness and endurance in the material. I explained to her that I only wanted to draw pictures on it, and that I did not want them to endure in the least; and that from my point of view, therefore, it was a question not of tough consistency, but of responsive surface, a thing comparatively irrelevant in a parcel. When she understood that I wanted to draw she offered to overwhelm me with note-paper, apparently supposing that I did my notes and correspondence on old brown paper wrappers from motives of economy.

I then tried to explain the rather delicate logical shade, that I not only like brown paper, but liked the quality of brownness in October woods, or in beer, or in the peat-streams of the North. Brown paper represents the primal twilight of the first toil of creation, and with a bright-coloured chalk or two you can pick out points of fire in it, sparks of gold, and blood-red, and sea-green, like the first fierce stars that sprang out of divine darkness. All this I said (in an off-hand way) to the old woman; and I put the brown paper in my pocket along with the chalks, and possibly other things. I suppose every one must have reflected how primeval and how poetical are the things that one carries in one's pocket; the pocket-knife, for instance, the type of all human tools, the infant of the sword. Once I planned to write a book of poems entirely about the things in my pocket. But I found it would be too long; and the age of great epics is past.

* * *

With my stick and my knife, my chalks and my brown paper, I went out on to the great downs. I crawled across those colossal contours that express the best quality of England, because they are at the same time soft and strong. The smoothness of them has the same meaning as the smoothness of great cart-horses, or the smoothness of the beech-tree; it declares in the teeth of our timid and cruel theories that the mighty are merciful. As my eye swept the landscape, the landscape was as kindly as any of its cottages, but for power it was like an earthquake. The villages in the immense valley were safe, one could see, for centuries; yet the lifting of the whole land was like the lifting of one enormous wave to wash them all away.

I crossed one swell of living turf after another, looking for a place to sit down and draw. Do not, for heaven's sake, imagine I was going to sketch from Nature. I was going to draw devils and seraphim, and blind old gods that men worshipped before the dawn of right, and saints in robes of angry crimson, and seas of strange green, and all the sacred or monstrous symbols that look so well in bright colours on brown paper. They are much better worth drawing than Nature; also they are much easier to draw. When a cow came slouching by in the field next to me, a mere artist might have drawn it; but I always get wrong in the hind legs of quadrupeds. So I drew the soul of the cow; which I saw there plainly walking before me in the sunlight; and the soul was all purple and silver, and had seven horns and the mystery that belongs to all the beasts. But though I could not with a crayon get the best out of the landscape, it does not follow that the landscape was not getting the best out of me. And this, I think, is the mistake that people make about the old poets who lived before Wordsworth, and were supposed not to care very much about Nature because they did not describe it much.

They preferred writing about great men to writing about great hills; but they sat on the great hills to write it. They gave out much less about Nature, but they drank in, perhaps, much more. They painted the white robes of their holy virgins with the blinding snow, at which they had stared all day. They blazoned the shields of their paladins with the purple and gold of many heraldic sunsets. The greenness of a thousand green leaves clustered into the live green figure of Robin Hood. The blueness of a score of forgotten skies became the blue robes of the Virgin. The inspiration went in like sunbeams and came out like Apollo.

*   *   *

But as I sat scrawling these silly figures on the brown paper, it began to dawn on me, to my great disgust, that I had left one chalk, and that a most exquisite and essential chalk, behind. I searched all my pockets, but I could not find any white chalk. Now, those who are acquainted with all the philosophy (nay, religion) which is typified in the art of drawing on brown paper, know that white is positive and essential. I cannot avoid remarking here upon a moral significance. One of the wise and awful truths which this brown-paper art reveals, is that, that white is a colour. It is not a mere absence of colour; it is a shining and affirmative thing, as fierce as red, as definite as black. When (so to speak) your pencil grows red-hot, it draws roses; when it grows white-hot, it draws stars. And one of the two or three defiant verities of the best religious morality, of real

Christianity for example, is exactly the same thing; the chief assertion of religious morality is that white is a colour. Virtue is not the absence of vices or the avoidance of moral dangers; virtue is a vivid and separate thing, like pain or a particular smell. Mercy does not mean not being cruel or sparing people revenge or punishment; it means a plain and positive thing like the sun, which one has either seen or not seen. Chastity does not mean abstention from sexual wrong; it means something flaming, like Joan of Arc. In a word, God paints in many colours; but He never paints so gorgeously, I had almost said so gaudily, as when He paints in white. In a sense our age has realized this fact, and expressed it in our sullen costume. For if it were really true that white was a blank and colourless thing, negative and non-committal, then white would be used instead of black and grey for the funeral dress of this pessimistic period. We should see city gentlemen in frock coats of spotless silver satin, with top hats as white as wonderful arum lilies. Which is not the case.

Meanwhile I could not find my chalk.

*   *   *

I sat on the hill in a sort of despair. There was no town nearer than Chichester at which it was even remotely probable that there would be such a thing as an artist's colourman. And yet, without white, my absurd little pictures would be as pointless as the world would be if there were no good people in it. I stared stupidly round, racking my brain for expedients. Then I suddenly stood up and roared with laughter, again and again, so that the cows stared at me and called a committee. Imagine a man in the Sahara regretting that he had no sand for his hourglass. Imagine a gentleman in mid-ocean wishing that he had brought some salt water with him for his chemical experiments. I was sitting on an immense warehouse of white chalk. The landscape was made entirely out of white chalk. White chalk was piled mere miles until it met the sky. I stooped and broke a piece off the rock I sat on: it did not mark so well as the shop chalks do; but it gave the effect. And I stood there in a trance of pleasure, realizing that this Southern England is not only a grand peninsula, and a tradition and a civilization; it is something even more admirable. It is a piece of chalk.

MARY WEBB

(1881–1927)

The Beauty of Shadow

'They seated themselves under the shade
of this white thorn, and took their solace.'
OLD ROMANCE

SHADOW is one of the easiest to perceive of all nature's
beauties. As one may see the charm of a profile for the
first time when looking at a silhouette, so one becomes
aware of the perfection of a natural outline more quickly
by seeing it drawn in one colour. It is much simpler to
trace the fairy fretwork of a mountain ash when it lies
on the grass in shadow than when the eyes are dazzled
by the vivid green and clustering scarlet of berry and
leaf against the sky. It has become a blue tree on the
green canvas of a field. Without shadow things would
seem unreal, unbreathing as figures in a dream—flat, un-
relieved tapestry on the walls of the world. With it come
reality and rounded loveliness. It is only the bare winter
tree, the barren heart, that are shadowless.

The colours of shadows vary with climate and season;
they are mauve on ripe corn, deeply black on hot, white
roads in summer, purple on ploughlands in sandstone

country, silver-grey on snow. Blue is their prevailing colour, varying from the sapphire of love-in-a-mist to the indigo at the root of a thundercloud.

In motion as well as in tint these astral bodies of material things have an ever-changing individuality— faithfully following or waiting beside their prototypes. They flit with the birds, small winged spirits, and even a bee's wing, so unsubstantial itself, has a faint replica that follows its airy fanning. The shade of a leaf caresses its own flower and its fellow-leaf with gentle strokings; and when a cherry blossom falls down the chequered steeps of the tree, a little mournful shadow goes with her. The shade of the tendrilled creeper steals into a room and lies along the floor, an emissary from the plant outside that peers in but cannot enter. The somnolent gloom thrown by the massed foliage gives majesty to the summer field; and how splendid, on some loud day in the equinox, is the sight of the dumb shadows of the shouting, gesticulating trees, tossing and bending, lengthening and shrinking over the land. Cloud-shadows on a plain are inexpressibly alluring. Some are like a mere breath on a mirror; others are dark and ominous, passing into the distance only to be replaced by fresh phalanxes, as though some conquering army had gone forth. But they are most stately over mountains, for they alone have power to darken the everlasting summits.

Midday, the period of practicality, is fitly unshadowed; perhaps that is why it has so little glamour. But when the tired labourer turns homeward in the evening, he is led or followed by a lengthening shade; every tree and hedge sends forth a little mimic to join the ranks; the sheep and cattle walk the fields with shapes of primeval beasts behind them; houses stand half-circled in black moats; the world is barred with gold and purple. Now beside the runlets on the hills the pipkins of the mimulus, which have stood half full of shadow all day, brim over. Now the sharp, clear outline of the western hill steadily ascends its neighbour, till all the heather has been quenched except the one line of blood-red at the summit; the thick curtain covers that also, but it has no power over the immortal heavens. Then comes sleep, and deepens down the world. Out of shadow comes the dewy morning; into it retires the silent dusk. Out of it, one by one, we wander, our young eyes full of mystery; into it we all depart, when the noonday heat is past and the labourer turns home.

If you go out on some June morning, before the earliest bee comes droning by, when the stripes of sunrise lie right across the awakening earth, you will know the fascination of shadows. On such a day they are almost as blue as chicory. As a child, I remember standing awe-stricken at the strange beauty of a well-known field in the magic of a June dawn. It had a line of tall trees in its eastern hedge, and if you watched while the sun rose, you saw what had been a wide, grey expanse suddenly spanned by swart, prostrate giants. It was as if, with one movement, every tree had flung itself upon its face—Mahommedan-wise—at the muezzin of sunrise. Perhaps the memory of such fresh delights, like dew in the flower-cup of life, may linger even after the flower is gathered. Quite early on a summer morning, if you look down an ugly street in a busy town, you will scarcely know it. The rows of houses have ceased to look dull, and have become the opposing camps of light and darkness; the street is a tessellated pavement of blue and yellow; the bush that looks so pathetically inadequate by day throws quite a forest of obscurity and becomes mysterious.

The shadow of a tree upon any house blesses it, weaving with its cool, hypnotic gestures a soothing quiet; but the place, of all human habitations, where it best loves to linger is a village street. There each life is framed in garden and orchard; companies of spirit-shapes go trembling up and down the humble walls and roofs all day from the multitude of surrounding leaves; in the highway the sunshine sleeps by the shadow of an ivied wall—disturbed only once in an hour, and then simply turning in its sleep. If those other shades, the troubles of life, have become too dense and shouldered out the light, so that the sick imagination sees them as crouching beasts of prey, a pilgrimage to such a tranquil place in lilac time may help to set things right again. In that sequestered road, where the whirr of a linnet's flight is startling, before the first workman comes through the dew, you can hardly fail to gather some share of peace. There, where the wet lilacs fling their fragrance from garden to garden like bridges, and the pale images of their massed blossom and heart-shaped leaves lie all along the way, questionings will seem a little unimportant— the shade-strewn road preaches so sweetly the necessity of interspersed dimness and light. By and by a door opens,

and a labourer goes whistling down the chequered track
that is so like his life. Here, even death loses some of its
grimness—its hideousness of association, which is so un-
necessary. For the imagination sees the highway of mortal
existence where it ends abruptly, penumbrous, flecked
with shade from the heart-shaped leaves of the Tree of
Life: and the shadow is the sign that we have come at
last within the pale of the tree's mysterious whisperings.

The slightly blurred colours of reflections—water-
shadows—are more vivid than reality, as if water were a
brighter medium than air; what they lose in strength of
outline through the motion of the current, they gain in
dreamy charm. Were ever forget-me-nots half so blue as
those that gaze skyward from clear water? Did you
know all the sweetness of flushed wild-rose faces until
you saw them sleeping in a stream? Some spell lies on
rivers where willows bend over them and transfuse them
with tender green, with depths of swaying leaf-reflections,
lighter in the centre, where the over-hanging tracery
shows the sky, very dark at the sides, where the grassy
banks are steep and the leaves thick. Such beauty brings
the longing (almost a torment to some minds) to be
absorbed in nature, dissolved in it even to the losing of
personality. Perhaps the person who most nearly ap-
proaches this oneness physically is a boy who plunges into
a green pool in the early morning. Spiritually, the Greeks
came near it, with their legends of maidens melting into
laurels or becoming nightingales after death. Beside a
full-flowing river in autumn this longing is strong and
urgent. Coming round a curve, you stop with a sudden

intake of the breath, dazzled by a blaze of glory. There stands on the bank and there lies in the flood a tree of beaten gold, gently moving against the sky, gently quivering in the water, flinging largess of its yellow money into the vistaed gold of its reflection. The sun makes each leaf transparent, and the whole picture is ardent as the face of some angel of a flaming star. As the spirit strives to gather some of the beauty, it longs to be less finite, less bounded; it desires an infinite future in which to reflect universal loveliness.

When the sun and the wind are abroad together, watch the cloud-reflections hurrying along with the current of a river, or travelling up-stream. This last is like the striving of two wills for the mastery; the froth of the current and the foam of the clouds continually cross.

In glassy lakes the surrounding woods meet in the depths of the water, and make a strange, new world. No wonder there are so many legends of villages and churches under meres, and bells ringing eerily below the water-lilies. Looking down into the limpid quiet, where everything is so familiar, yet so alien, the eye sees, beyond those mysterious green glades, habitations of the water-country, twisted of chimney as an elfin chateau, blurred replicas of some cottage on the bank, wavering in outline and impossible in perspective. Almost one can see the inhabitants passing at the end of the glades, or a white hand waving from the window of an unsubstantial dwelling. Almost one can see the gleaming arm of some water-maiden—Aigle or Vivian of the Lake—beckoning, bare and beautiful, or clad in shining samite. Though there is no Hylas now to be charmed into the green silence, no Excalibur to be lifted above the mere, yet there is still magic in these reflections.

On calm, hot days, water sends up over bank and tree vacillating, shimmering patterns that waver to the tree-top and back again, like flocks of hovering golden birds. Far within clear water dwells the sun's twin brother; there the pale sister of the moon goes sailing; there the stars glimmer, spreading into little moons, shrinking into mere points of light at the will of the water.

When we look down into the blueness of some little pool, rejoicing in the birdlike passage of the clouds, and then look up to the wide sky, we realize that the finite is like a lake which, as far as its capacity allows, mirrors the infinite; and when we see the foreshortened image of a poplar stretched in pale colouring beneath it, we have a sudden vision of time as the faint, straitened shadow of eternity.

HENRY BESTON

(1888–   )

The Headlong Wave

THIS morning I am going to try my hand at something that I do not recall ever having encountered either in a periodical or in a book, namely, a chapter on the ways, the forms, and the sounds of ocean near a beach. Friends are forever asking me about the surf on the great beach and if I am not sometimes troubled or haunted by its sound. To this I reply that I have grown unconscious of the roar, and though it sounds all day long in my waking ears, and all night long in my sleeping ones, my ears seldom send on the long tumult to the mind. I hear the roar the instant I wake in the morning and return to consciousness, I listen to it a while consciously, and then accept and forget it; I hear it during the day only when I stop again to listen, or when some change in the nature of the sound breaks through my acceptance of it to my curiosity.

They say here that great waves reach this coast in threes. Three great waves, then an indeterminate run of lesser rhythms, then three great waves again. On Celtic coasts it is the seventh wave that is seen coming like a king out of the gray, cold sea. The Cape tradition, however, is no half-real, half-mystical fancy, but the truth itself. Great waves do indeed approach this beach by threes. Again and again have I watched three giants roll in one after the other out of the Atlantic, cross the outer bar, break, form again, and follow each other in to fulfillment and destruction on this solitary beach. Coast guard crews are all well aware of this triple rhythm and take advantage of the lull that follows the last wave to launch their boats.

It is true that there are single giants as well. I have been roused by them in the night. Waked by their tremendous and unexpected crash, I have sometimes heard the last of the heavy overspill, sometimes only the loud, withdrawing roar. After the roar came a briefest pause, and after the pause the return of ocean to the night's long cadences. Such solitary titans, flinging their green tons down upon a quiet world, shake beach and dune. Late one September night, as I sat reading, the very father of all waves must have flung himself down before the house, for the quiet of the night was suddenly overturned by a gigantic, tumbling crash and an earthquake rumbling; the beach trembled beneath the avalanche, the dune shook, and my house so shook in its dune that the flame of a lamp quivered and pictures jarred on the wall.

The three great elemental sounds in nature are the sound of rain, the sound of wind in a primeval wood, and the sound of outer ocean on a beach. I have heard them all, and of the three elemental voices, that of ocean is the most awesome, beautiful, and varied. For it is a mistake to talk of the monotone of ocean or of the monotonous nature of its sound. The sea has many voices. Listen to the surf, really lend it your ears, and you will hear in it a world of sounds: hollow boomings and heavy roarings, great watery tumblings and tramplings, long hissing seethes, sharp, rifle-shot reports, splashes, whispers, the grinding undertone of stones, and sometimes vocal sounds that might be the half-heard talk of people in the sea. And not only is the great sound varied in the manner of its making, it is also constantly changing its tempo, its pitch, its accent, and its rhythm, being now loud and thundering, now almost placid, now furious, now grave and solemn-slow, now a simple measure, now a rhythm monstrous with a sense of purpose and elemental will.

Every mood of the wind, every change in the day's weather, every phase of the tide—all these have subtle sea music all their own. Surf of the ebb, for instance, is one music, surf of the flood another, the change in the two musics being most clearly marked during the first hour of a rising tide. With the renewal of the tidal energy, the sound of the surf grows louder, the fury of battle returns to it as it turns again on the land, and beat and sound change with the renewal of the war.

Sound of surf in these autumnal dunes—the continuousness of it, sound of endless charging, endless incoming and gathering, endless fulfillment and dissolution, endless fecundity, and endless death. I have been trying to study out the mechanics of that mighty resonance. The dominant note is the great spilling crash made by each arriving wave. It may be hollow and booming, it may be heavy and churning, it may be a tumbling roar. The second fundamental sound is the wild seething cataract roar of the wave's dissolution and the rush of its foaming waters up the beach—this second sound *diminuendo*. The third fundamental sound is the endless dissolving hiss of the inmost slides of foam. The first two sounds reach the ear as a unisonance—the booming impact of the tons of water and the wild roar of the up-rush blending—and this mingled sound dissolves into the foam-bubble hissing of the third. Above the tumult, like birds, fly wisps of watery noise, splashes and counter splashes, whispers, seething, slaps, and chucklings. An overtone sound of other breakers, mingled with a general rumbling, fills earth and sea and air.

Here do I pause to warn my reader that although I have recounted the history of a breaker—an ideal breaker—the surf process must be understood as mingled and continuous, waves hurrying after waves, interrupting waves, washing back on waves, overwhelming waves. Moreover, I have described the sound of a high surf in fair weather. A storm surf is mechanically the same thing, but it *grinds*, and this same long, sepulchral grinding—sound of utter terror to all mariners—is a development of the second fundamental sound; it is the cry of the breaker water roaring its way ashore and dragging at the sand. A strange underbody of sound when heard through the high, wild screaming of a gale.

Breaking waves that have to run up a steep tilt of the beach are often followed by a dragging, grinding sound—the note of the baffled water running downhill again to the sea. It is loudest when the tide is low and breakers are rolling beach stones up and down a slope of the lower beach.

I am, perhaps, most conscious of the sound of surf just

after I have gone to bed. Even here I read myself to drowsiness, and, reading, I hear the cadenced trampling roar filling all the dark. So close is the fo'castle to the ocean's edge that the rhythm of sound I hear oftenest in fair weather is not so much a general tumult as an endless arrival, overspill, and dissolution of separate great seas. Through the dark, mathematic square of the screened half window, I listen to the rushes and the bursts, the tramplings, and the long, intermingled thunderings, never wearying of the sonorous and universal sound.

Away from the beach, the various sounds of the surf melt into one great thundering symphonic roar. Autumnal nights in Eastham village are full of this ocean sound. The "summer people" have gone, the village rests and prepares for winter, lamps shine from kitchen windows; and from across the moors, the great levels of the marsh, and the bulwark of the dunes resounds the long wintry roaring of the sea. Listen to it a while, and it will seem but one remote and formidable sound; listen still longer and you will discern in it a symphony of breaker thunderings, an endless, distant, elemental cannonade. There is beauty in it, and ancient terror. I heard it last as I walked through the village on a starry October night; there was no wind, the leafless trees were still, all the village was abed, and the whole somber world was awesome with the sound.

ROBERT LYND

(1879–1949)

The Pleasures of Ignorance

IT IS impossible to take a walk in the country with an average townsman—especially, perhaps, in April or May —without being amazed at the vast continent of his ignorance. It is impossible to take a walk in the country oneself without being amazed at the vast continent of one's own ignorance. Thousands of men and women live and die without knowing the difference between a beech and an elm, between the song of a thrush and the song of a blackbird. Probably in a modern city the man who can distinguish between a thrush's and a blackbird's song is the exception. It is not that we have not seen the birds. It is simply that we have not noticed them. We have been surrounded by birds all our lives, yet so feeble is our observation that many of us could not tell whether or not the chaffinch sings, or the colour of the cuckoo. We argue like small boys as to whether the cuckoo always sings as he flies or sometimes in the branches of a tree—whether Chapman drew on his fancy or his knowledge of nature in the lines:

> *When in the oak's green arms the cuckoo sings,*
> *And first delights men in the lovely springs.*

This ignorance, however, is not altogether miserable. Out of it we get the constant pleasure of discovery. Every fact of nature comes to us each spring, if only we are sufficiently ignorant, with the dew still on it. If we have lived half a lifetime without having ever seen a cuckoo, and know it only as a wondering voice, we are all the more delighted at the spectacle of its runaway flight as it hurries from wood to wood conscious of its crimes and at the way in which it halts hawk-like in the wind, its long tail quivering, before it dares descend on a hillside of fir-trees where avenging presences may lurk. It would be absurd to pretend that the naturalist does not also find pleasure in observing the life of the birds, but his is a steady pleasure, almost a sober and plodding occupation, compared to the morning enthusiasm of the man who sees a cuckoo for the first time, and, behold, the world is made new.

And, as to that, the happiness even of the naturalist depends in some measure upon his ignorance, which still leaves him new worlds of this kind to conquer. He may have reached the very Z of knowledge in the books, but he still feels half ignorant until he has confirmed each bright particular with his eyes. He wishes with his own eyes to see the female cuckoo—rare spectacle!—as she lays her egg on the ground and takes it in her bill to the nest in which it is destined to breed infanticide. He would sit day after day with a field-glass against his eyes in order personally to endorse or refute the evidence suggesting that the cuckoo *does* lay on the ground and not in a nest. And, if he is so far fortunate as to discover this most secretive of birds in the very act of laying, there still remain for him other fields to conquer in a multitude of such disputed questions as whether the cuckoo's egg is always of the same colour as the other eggs in the nest in which she abandons it. Assuredly the men of science have no reason as yet to weep over their lost ignorance. If they seem to know everything, it is only because you and I know almost nothing. There will always be a fortune of ignorance waiting for them under every fact they turn up. They will never know what song the Sirens sang to Ulysses any more than Sir Thomas Browne did.

If I have called in the cuckoo to illustrate the ordinary man's ignorance, it is not because I can speak with authority on that bird. It is simply because, passing the spring in a parish that seemed to have been invaded by all the cuckoos of Africa, I realized how exceedingly little I, or anybody else I met, knew about them. But your and my ignorance is not confined to cuckoos. It dabbles in all created things, from the sun and moon down to the names of the flowers. I once heard a clever lady asking whether the new moon always appears on the same day of the week. She added that perhaps it is better not to know, because, if one does not know when or in what part of the sky to expect it, its appearance is always a pleasant surprise. I fancy, however, the new moon always comes as a surprise even to those who are familiar with her time-tables. And it is the same with the coming-in of spring and the waves of the flowers. We are not the less delighted to find an early primrose because we are sufficiently learned in the services of the year to look for it in March or April rather than in October. We know, again, that the blossom precedes and not succeeds the fruit of the apple-tree, but this does not lessen our amazement at the beautiful holiday of a May orchard.

At the same time there is, perhaps, a special pleasure in relearning the names of many of the flowers every spring. It is like rereading a book that one has almost forgotten. Montaigne tells us that he had so bad a memory that he could always read an old book as though he had never read it before. I have myself a capricious and leaking memory. I can read *Hamlet* itself and *The Pickwick Papers* as though they were the work of new authors and had come wet from the press, so much of them fades between one reading and another. There are occasions on which a memory of this kind is an affliction, especially if one has a passion for accuracy. But this is only when life has an object beyond entertainment. In respect of mere luxury, it may be doubted whether there is not as much to be said for a bad memory as for a good one. With a bad memory one can go on reading Plutarch and *The Arabian Nights* all one's life. Little shreds and tags, it is probable, will stick even in the worst memory, just as a succession of sheep cannot leap through a gap in a hedge without leaving a few wisps of wool on the thorns. But the sheep themselves escape, and the great authors leap in the same way out of an idle memory and leave little enough behind.

And, if we can forget books, it is as easy to forget the months and what they showed us, when once they are gone. Just for a moment I tell myself that I know May like the multiplication table and could pass an examination on its flowers, their appearance and their order. Today I can

affirm confidently that the buttercup has five petals. (Or is
it six? I knew for certain last week.) But next year I shall
probably have forgotten my arithmetic, and may have to
learn once more not to confuse the buttercup with the
celandine. Once more I shall see the world as a garden
through the eyes of a stranger, my breath taken away with
surprise by the painted fields. I shall find myself wondering whether it is science or ignorance which affirms that
the swift (that black exaggeration of the swallow and yet
a kinsman of the humming-bird) never settles even on a
nest, but disappears at night into the heights of the air. I
shall learn with fresh astonishment that it is the male, and
not the female, cuckoo that sings. I may have to learn again
not to call the campion a wild geranium, and to rediscover
whether the ash comes early or late in the etiquette of the
trees. A contemporary English novelist was once asked by
a foreigner what was the most important crop in England.
He answered without a moment's hesitation: "Rye." Ignorance so complete as this seems to me to be touched with
magnificence; but the ignorance even of illiterate persons
is enormous. The average man who uses a telephone could
not explain how a telephone works. He takes for granted
the telephone, the railway train, the linotype, the aero-
plane, as our grandfathers took for granted the miracles of
the gospels. He neither questions nor understands them. It
is as though each of us investigated and made his own only
a tiny circle of facts. Knowledge outside the day's work is
regarded by most men as a gewgaw. Still we are constantly
in reaction against our ignorance. We rouse ourselves at
intervals and speculate. We revel in speculations about

anything at all—about life after death or about such questions as that which is said to have puzzled Aristotle, "why sneezing from noon to midnight was good, but from night to noon unlucky." One of the greatest joys known to man is to take such a flight into ignorance in search of knowledge. The great pleasure of ignorance is, after all, the pleasure of asking questions. The man who has lost this pleasure or exchanged it for the pleasure of dogma, which is the pleasure of answering, is already beginning to stiffen. One envies so inquisitive a man as Jowett, who sat down to the study of physiology in his sixties. Most of us have lost the sense of our ignorance long before that age. We even become vain of our squirrel's hoard of knowledge and regard increasing age itself as a school of omniscience. We forget that Socrates was famed for wisdom not because he was omniscient but because he realized at the age of seventy that he still knew nothing.

DONALD CULROSS PEATTIE

(1898–   )

April Second

Each year, and above all, each spring, raises up for Nature a new generation of lovers—and this quite irrespective of the age of the new votary. As I write this a boy is going out to the marshes to watch with field glasses the mating of the red-winged blackbirds, rising up in airy swirls and clouds. Or perhaps he carries some manual to the field, and sits him down on an old log, to trace his way through Latin names, that seem at first so barbarous and stiff. There is no explaining why the boy has suddenly forsaken the ball and bat, or finds a kite less interesting in the spring skies than a bird. For a few weeks, or a few seasons, or perhaps for a lifetime, he will follow this bent with passion.

And at the same time there will be a man who all his life has put away this call, or never heard it before, who has come to the easier, latter end of life, when leisure is his own. And he goes out in the woods to collect his first botanical specimen and to learn that he has much to learn for all his years.

They are never to be forgotten—that first bird pursued

through thicket and over field with serious intent, not to
kill but to know it, or that first plant lifted reverently and
excitedly from the earth. No spring returns but that I wish
I might live again through the moment when I went out in
the woods and sat down with a book in my hands, to learn
not only the name, but the ways and the range and the
charm of the windflower, *Anemone quinquefolia.*

JOSEPH WOOD KRUTCH

(1893–   )

June—Spring Rain

ONE trouble with the city is that there is so much bad weather there. Nearly everybody admits that snow is merely an expensive nuisance, and even the early summer rains serve no real purpose where there is nothing to be watered and where sewers have to be built to drain the insipid liquid away. Some day, no doubt, when we have become thoroughly urbanized, whole areas will be roofed over and the ideal amount of ultraviolet supplied by electricity. Children can be taken occasionally to the country to see what the sun looks like as they are taken now to see a hill or a mountain. Probably many of them will not want to go anyway, for the country will be to them only what it was to the London club man: "A damp sort of place where all sorts of birds fly about uncooked." But that will be all right too—for those who like it.

The good thing about the country is, on the other hand, that we don't have there any bad weather at all—only a number of different kinds of good. In fact I should be willing to maintain that there, and there only, do we have what has any right to be called weather at all—as distinguished, I mean, from those mere inclemencies of one kind or another, which do no more than make the difference between a day when it is convenient to walk to the subway and one when the only choice is between getting messy and uncomfortable trying to walk, and getting equally messy and uncomfortable waiting for the taxi which, of course, some luckier people have already taken.

Sometimes, I will admit, even in the country we do have rather too much of one kind of good weather for too long at a time—as we have been having it just now when rain has been falling and falling and falling as though some sorcerer's apprentice had forgotten how to turn it off. Even the thirstiest flowers do not need that much water; they are in danger of being drowned out. And the situation inclines one to the suspicion that Nature is not, as some philosophers have insisted, a Golden Mean, but essentially intemperate, never knowing when to stop, whether it is in pouring down raindrops or multiplying seed. At least the living things seem to go on getting bigger and more numerous and more extravagant until something not themselves puts a stop to it.

I have never lived long enough in England to get the real English point of view which expresses itself when the countryman looks out of the window at the steady sleety drizzle and says—as I have heard him say in all seriousness —"What a lovely day for a walk!" I do go out in the rain from time to time but not for long, and I conclude somewhat pusillanimously that this kind of good weather is enjoyed best when looked at through a window rather than when actually participated in.

Thank goodness I do not feel any obligation to do what some people call "catching up with their reading"—which means, generally, reading the things they don't want to read but do at least skim through, because someone is going to ask them about the latest novel, or even perhaps discover that the *Odyssey* is for them, literally, a closed book. But notoriously a rainy day is a good time to read and I do read a little bit of everything, including the works of those who have tried before me to get down on paper a hint of what the privilege of living with some awareness of other living things has meant to them.

*   *   *

"There was never yet," of course, "philosopher that could endure the toothache patiently." If this spring rain were a hurricane, even if the water should get too seriously into my basement, I should soon enough begin to lose my serenity and to see the thing *sub specie temporis*. So far, however, the basement is dry and there is no immediate prospect that the price of vegetables will rise still further as the result of too wet a season. I am still, therefore, a philosopher. The rain, I can still say a bit smugly, falleth upon the just and the unjust. It has no intentions. It is good for those who can take some advantage of it; bad for those for whom it will drown or rot. "The stars are little twinkling rogues who light us home sometimes when we are drunk but care for neither you nor me nor any man." I can, in other words, if not accept the universe, then at least accept that small part of it which is calling my attention to itself at the moment.

FREEMAN TILDEN

(1883–   )

Interlude

(Afternoon in late June at Acadia National Park)

ONE of the many sylvan footpaths and fire-control roads passes a swampy pond, a glacial remnant on its way to becoming dry land in time, but there is shallow water with lush vegetation in plenty still. Somebody has dumped gravel to make a dry-shod approach to the water's edge. The round-leaf sundew has come up through the gravel and sets a snare with its sticky leaves for tiny insects. Over at one side of the footway a single pitcher plant, the Jedediah Smith of the plant-trappers, rears its head from the water. Behind it a pair of inquiring eyes is fixed on me—those of a frog that just dunked in.

The air is bland, but a faint breeze has zest in it, and in the open spaces among the reedy growth the sky-blue reflections are rippled. The stickwork of a beaver dam is out just in front of me. I watch awhile for a beaver to appear, but none comes. Behind me in a natural plantation of poplar I have already seen where these tireless and inventive woodsmen have been at work. Dozens of trees as big through as my upper arm show the neat chiseling of the teeth. It is not the way I cut down trees myself. The bottom end of the felled trees is a cone; and where the beaver has left his felling job unfinished, the cut is in the shape of an hourglass. I fall awondering at just which point in the cutting the animal dodges and gets from under. I lingered too long once. I still possess a scar.

Something comes swimming straight toward me: a muskrat, making good time, half out of water, with easy strokes. He finally sees me standing there, jams his rudder hard aport, and without too much concern sets a course straight back again. There are plenty of birds flitting about, but they are unusually quiet—a chip here and a twitter there.

Nothing exciting happens. The surrounding hills shimmer a little in a filmy haze. I come away from the spot with a pleasant feeling of partnership in all the small business transactions of the world. Several thousands of eyes have been looking at me all the while—little lives I could not see with mine. I am not a naturalist. My perception misses a good deal. I do not flatter myself that any of the creatures has overrated me; not even that they had any keen interest in me. Yet I do have the agreeable sensation that I have not, as a guest, been unwelcome.

It is now three days since I saw a newspaper headline. I feel relaxed. A little swampy pond in a national park can be a healing thing, I find.

✳ PART III ✳

TRAVELING

FRANCIS BACON

(1561–1626)

Of Travel

Travel, in the younger sort, is a part of education; in the elder, a part of experience. He that travelleth into a country, before he hath some entrance into the language, goeth to school and not to travel. That young men travel under some tutor or grave servant, I allow well; so that he be such a one that hath the language, and hath been in the country before; whereby he may be able to tell them what things are worthy to be seen in the country where they go, what acquaintances they are to seek, what exercises or discipline the place yieldeth; for else young men shall go hooded, and look abroad little.

It is a strange thing, that in sea voyages, where there is nothing to be seen but sky and sea, men should make diaries; but in land travel, wherein so much is to be observed, for the most part they omit it; as if chance were fitter to be registered than observation: let diaries, therefore, be brought in use. The things to be seen and observed are, the courts of princes, especially when they give audience to ambassadors; the courts of justice, while they sit and hear causes; and so of consistories ecclesiastic; the churches and monasteries, with the monuments which are therein extant; the walls and fortifications of cities and towns; and so the havens and harbours, antiquities and ruins, libraries, colleges, disputations, and lectures, where any are; shipping and navies; houses and gardens of state and pleasure, near great cities; armories, arsenals, magazines, exchanges, burses, warehouses, exercises of horsemanship, fencing, training of soldiers, and the like: comedies, such whereunto the better sort of persons do resort; treasuries of jewels and robes; cabinets and rarities; and, to conclude, whatsoever is memorable in the places where they go; after all which the tutors or servants ought to make diligent inquiry. As for triumphs, masks, feasts, weddings, funerals, capital executions, and such shows, men need not to be put in mind of them: yet are they not to be neglected.

If you will have a young man to put his travel into a little room, and in short time to gather much, this you must do: first, as was said, he must have some entrance into the language before he goeth; then he must have such a servant, or tutor, as knoweth the country, as was likewise said: let him carry with him also some card, or book, describing the country where he travelleth, which will be a good key to his inquiry; let him keep also a diary; let him not stay long in one city or town, more or less as the place deserveth, but not long; nay, when he stayeth in one city or town, let him change his lodging from one end and part of the town to another, which is a great adamant of acquaintance; let him sequester himself from the company of his countrymen, and diet in such places where there is good company of the nation where he travelleth: let him, upon his removes from one place to another, procure recommendation to some person of quality residing in the place whither he removeth, that he may use his favour in those things he desireth to see or know; thus he may abridge his travel with much profit.

As for the acquaintance which is to be sought in travel, that which is most of all profitable, is acquaintance with the secretaries and employed men of ambassadors; for so in travelling in one country he shall suck the experience of many: let him also see and visit eminent persons in all kinds, which are of great name abroad, that he may be able to tell how the life agreeth with the fame; for quarrels, they are with care and discretion to be avoided; they are commonly for mistresses, healths, place and words; and let a man beware how he keepeth company with choleric and quarrelsome persons; for they will engage him into their own quarrels. When a traveller returneth home, let him not leave the countries where he hath travelled altogether behind him, but maintain a correspondence by letters with those of his acquaintance which are of most worth; and let his travel appear rather in his discourse than in his apparel or gesture; and in his discourse let him be rather advised in his answers, than forward to tell stories: and let it appear that he doth not change his country manners for those of foreign parts; but only prick in some flowers of that he hath learned abroad into the customs of his own country.

JOSEPH ADDISON

(1672–1719)

The Tombs in Westminster Abbey

W<small>HEN</small> I am in a serious humour, I very often walk by myself in Westminster Abbey; where the gloominess of the place, and the use to which it is applied, with the solemnity of the building, and the condition of the people who lie in it, are apt to fill the mind with a kind of melancholy, or rather thoughtfulness, that is not disagreeable. I yesterday passed a whole afternoon in the churchyard, the cloisters, and the church, amusing myself with the tombstones and inscriptions that I met with in those several regions of the dead. Most of them recorded nothing else of the buried person but that he was born upon one day and died upon another: the whole history of his life being comprehended in those two circumstances that are common to all mankind.

I could not but look upon these registers of existence, whether of brass or marble, as a kind of satire upon the departed persons; who had left no other memorial of them, but that they were born and that they died. They put me in mind of several persons mentioned in the battles of heroic poems, who have sounding names given them for no

other reason but that they may be killed, and are celebrated
for nothing but being knocked on the head. The life of
these men is finely described in Holy Writ by the path of
an arrow, which is immediately closed up and lost.

Upon my going into the church, I entertained myself
with the digging of a grave; and saw in every shovelful of
it that was thrown up, the fragment of a bone or skull in-
termixed with a kind of fresh mouldering earth that some
time or other had a place in the composition of a human
body. Upon this I began to consider with myself what
innumerable multitudes of people lay confused together
under the pavement of that ancient cathedral; how men
and women, friends and enemies, priests and soldiers,
monks and prebendaries, were crumbled amongst one another, and blended together in the same common mass; how
beauty, strength, and youth, with old age, weakness, and
deformity, lay undistinguished in the same promiscuous
heap of matter.

After having thus surveyed this great magazine of mor-
tality, as it were in the lump, I examined it more particularly by the accounts which I found on several of the
monuments which are raised in every quarter of that ancient fabric. Some of them were covered with such extravagant epitaphs that, if it were possible for the dead person to be acquainted with them, he would blush at the
praises which his friends have bestowed upon him. There
are others so excessively modest that they deliver the character of the person departed in Greek or Hebrew, and by
that means are not understood once in a twelve-month. In
the poetical quarter, I found there were poets who had no

monuments, and monuments which had no poets. I observed indeed that the present war had filled the church with many of these uninhabited monuments, which had been erected to the memory of persons whose bodies were perhaps buried in the plains of Blenheim, or in the bosom of the ocean.

I could not but be very much delighted with several modern epitaphs, which are written with great elegance of expression and justness of thought, and therefore do honour to the living as well as to the dead. As a foreigner is very apt to conceive an idea of the ignorance or politeness of a nation from the turn of their public monuments and inscriptions, they should be submitted to the perusal of men of learning and genius before they are put in execution. Sir Cloudesley Shovel's monument has very often given me great offence. Instead of the brave, rough English admiral, which was the distinguishing character of that plain, gallant man, he is represented on his tomb by the figure of a beau, dressed in a long periwig, and reposing himself upon velvet cushions under a canopy of state. The inscription is answerable to the monument, for instead of celebrating the many remarkable actions he had performed in the service of his country, it acquaints us only with the manner of his death, in which it was impossible for him to reap any honour. The Dutch, whom we are apt to despise for want of genius, show an infinitely greater taste of antiquity and politeness in their buildings and works of this nature, than what we meet with in those of our own country. The monuments of their admirals, which have been erected at a public expense, represent them like themselves, and are adorned with rostral crowns and naval ornaments, with beautiful festoons of seaweed, shells, and coral.

But to return to our subject. I have left the repository of our English kings for the contemplation of another day, when I shall find my mind disposed for so serious an amusement. I know that entertainments of this nature are apt to raise dark and dismal thoughts in timorous minds and gloomy imaginations; but for my own part, though I am always serious, I do not know what it is to be melancholy, and can therefore take a view of nature in her deep and solemn scenes, with the same pleasure as in her most gay and delightful ones. By this means, I can improve myself with those objects which others consider with terror.

When I look upon the tombs of the great, every emotion of envy dies in me; when I read the epitaphs of the beautiful, every inordinate desire goes out; when I meet with the grief of parents upon a tombstone, my heart melts with compassion; when I see the tomb of the parents themselves, I consider the vanity of grieving for those whom we must quickly follow; when I see kings lying by those who deposed them, when I consider rival wits placed side by side, or the holy men that divided the world with their contests and disputes, I reflect with sorrow and astonishment on the little competitions, factions, and debates of mankind. When I read the several dates of the tombs—of some that died yesterday, and some six hundred years ago—I consider that great day when we shall all of us be contemporaries, and make our appearance together.

WASHINGTON IRVING

(1783–1859)

The Balcony

I HAVE spoken of a balcony of the central window of the Hall of Ambassadors. It served as a kind of observatory, where I used often to take my seat, and consider not merely the heaven above but the earth beneath. Besides the magnificent prospect which it commanded of mountain, valley, and Vega, there was a little busy scene of human life laid open to inspection immediately below. At the foot of the hill was an *alameda*, or public walk, which, though not so fashionable as the more modern and splendid *paseo* of the Xenil, still boasted a varied and picturesque concourse. Hither resorted the small gentry of the suburbs, together with priests and friars, who walked for appetite and digestion; *majos* and *majas*, the beaux and belles of the lower classes, in their Andalusian dresses; swaggering *contrabandistas*, and sometimes half-muffled and mysterious loungers of the higher ranks, on some secret assignation.

It was a moving picture of Spanish life and character, which I delighted to study; and as the astronomer has his grand telescope with which to sweep the skies, and, as it were, bring the stars nearer for his inspection, so I had a smaller one, of pocket size, for the use of my observatory, with which I could sweep the regions below, and bring the countenances of the motley groups so close as almost, at times, to make me think I could divine their conversation by the play and expression of their features. I was thus, in a manner, an invisible observer, and, without quitting my solitude, could throw myself in an instant into the midst of society,—a rare advantage to one of somewhat shy and quiet habits, and fond, like myself, of observing the drama of life without becoming an actor in the scene.

There was a considerable suburb lying below the Alhambra, filling the narrow gorge of the valley, and extending up the opposite hill of the Albaycin. Many of the houses were built in the Moorish style, round *patios*, or courts, cooled by fountains and open to the sky; and as the inhabitants passed much of their time in these courts, and on the terraced roofs during the summer season, it follows that many a glance of their domestic life might be obtained by an aërial spectator like myself, who could look down on them from the clouds.

I enjoyed in some degree the advantages of the student in the famous old Spanish story, who beheld all Madrid unroofed for his inspection; and my gossiping squire, Mateo Ximenes, officiated occasionally as my Asmodeus, to give me anecdotes of the different mansions and their inhabitants.

I preferred, however, to form conjectural histories for myself, and thus would sit for hours, weaving, from casual incidents and indications passing under my eye, a whole tissue of schemes, intrigues, and occupations of the busy mortals below. There was scarce a pretty face or a striking figure that I daily saw, about which I had not thus gradually framed a dramatic story, though some of my characters would occasionally act in direct opposition to the part assigned them, and disconcert the whole drama. Reconnoitring one day with my glass the streets of the Albaycin, I beheld the procession of a novice about to take the veil; and remarked several circumstances which excited the strongest sympathy in the fate of the youthful being thus about to be consigned to a living tomb. I ascertained to my satisfaction that she was beautiful, and, from the paleness of her cheek, that she was a victim rather than a votary. She was arrayed in bridal garments, and decked with a chaplet of white flowers, but her heart evidently revolted at this mockery of a spiritual union, and yearned after its earthly loves. A tall stern-looking man walked near her in the procession: it was, of course, the tyrannical father, who, from some bigoted or sordid motive, had compelled this sacrifice. Amid the crowd was a dark handsome youth, in Andalusian garb, who seemed to fix on her an eye of agony. It was doubtless the secret lover from whom she was for ever to be separated. My indignation rose as I noted the malignant expression painted on the countenances of the attendant monks and friars. The procession arrived at the chapel of the convent; the sun gleamed for the last time upon the chaplet of the poor novice, as she crossed the fatal threshold and disappeared within the building. The throng poured in with cowl, and cross, and minstrelsy; the lover paused for a moment at the door. I could divine the tumult of his feelings; but he mastered them, and entered. There was a long interval. I pictured to myself the scene passing within: the poor novice despoiled of her transient finery, and clothed in the conventual garb; the bridal chaplet taken from her brow, and her beautiful head shorn of its long silken tresses. I heard her murmur the irrevocable vow. I saw her extended on a bier; the deathpall spread over her; the funeral service performed that proclaimed her dead to the world; her sighs were drowned in the deep tones of the organ, and the plaintive requiem of the nuns; the father looked on, unmoved, without a tear; the lover—no—my imagination refused to portray the anguish of the lover—there the picture remained a blank.

After a time the throng again poured forth, and dispersed various ways, to enjoy the light of the sun and mingle with the stirring scenes of life; but the victim, with her bridal chaplet, was no longer there. The door of the convent closed that severed her from the world for ever. I saw the father and the lover issue forth; they were in earnest conversation. The latter was vehement in his gesticulations; I expected some violent termination to my drama; but an angle of a building interfered and closed the scene. My eye afterwards was frequently turned to that convent with painful interest. I remarked late at night a solitary light twinkling from a remote lattice of one of its towers. "There," said I, "the unhappy nun sits weeping in her cell, while perhaps her lover paces the street below in unavailing anguish."

The officious Mateo interrupted my meditations and destroyed in an instant the cobweb tissue of my fancy. With his usual zeal he had gathered facts concerning the scene, which put my fictions all to flight. The heroine of my romance was neither young nor handsome; she had no lover; she had entered the convent of her own free will, as a respectable asylum, and was one of the most cheerful residents within its walls.

It was some little while before I could forgive the wrong done me by the nun in being thus happy in her cell, in contradiction to all the rules of romance; I diverted my spleen, however, by watching, for a day or two, the pretty coquetries of a dark-eyed brunette, who, from the covert of a balcony shrouded with flowering shrubs and a silken awning, was carrying on a mysterious correspondence with a handsome, dark, well-whiskered cavalier, who lurked frequently in the street beneath her window. Sometimes I saw him at an early hour stealing forth wrapped to the eyes in a mantle. Sometimes he loitered at a corner, in various disguises, apparently waiting for a private signal to slip into the house. Then there was the tinkling of a guitar at night and a lantern shifted from place to place in the balcony. I imagined another intrigue like that of Almaviva, but was again disconcerted in all my suppositions. The supposed lover turned out to be the husband of the lady, and a noted *contrabandista;* and all his mysterious signs and movements had doubtless some smuggling scheme in view.

I occasionally amused myself with noting from this balcony the gradual changes of the scenes below, according to the different stages of the day.

Scarce has the gray dawn streaked the sky, and the earliest cock crowed from the cottages of the hill-side, when the suburbs give sign of reviving animation; for the fresh hours of dawning are precious in the summer season in a sultry climate. All are anxious to get the start of the sun, in the business of the day. The muleteer drives forth his loaded train for the journey; the traveller slings his carbine behind his saddle, and mounts his steed at the gate of the hostel; the brown peasant from the country urges forward his loitering beasts, laden with panniers of sunny fruit and fresh dewy vegetables, for already the thrifty housewives are hastening to the market.

The sun is up and sparkles along the valley, tipping the transparent foliage of the groves. The matin bells resound melodiously through the pure bright air, announcing the hour of devotion. The muleteer halts his burdened animals before the chapel, thrusts his staff through his belt behind, and enters with hat in hand, smoothing his coal-black hair to hear a mass, and to put up a prayer for a prosperous way-faring across the *sierra*. And now steals forth on fairy foot the gentle *señora*, in trim *basquiña*, with restless fan in hand, and dark eye flashing from beneath the gracefully folded mantilla; she seeks some well-frequented church to offer up her morning orisons; but the nicely adjusted dress, the dainty shoe and cobweb stocking, the raven tresses exquisitely braided, the fresh-plucked rose, gleaming among them like a gem, show that earth divides with Heaven the empire of her thoughts. Keep an eye upon her, careful mother, or virgin aunt, or vigilant *duenna*, whichever you may be, that walk behind!

As the morning advances, the din of labour augments

on every side; the streets are thronged with man, and steed, and beast of burden, and there is a hum and murmur, like the surges of the ocean. As the sun ascends to his meridian, the hum and bustle gradually decline; at the height of noon there is a pause. The panting city sinks into lassitude, and for several hours there is a general repose. The windows are closed, the curtains drawn, the inhabitants retire into the coolest recesses of their mansions; the full-fed monk snores in his dormitory; the brawny porter lies stretched on the pavement beside his burden; the peasant and the labourer sleep beneath the trees of the Alameda, lulled by the sultry chirping of the locust. The streets are deserted, except by the water-carrier, who refreshes the ear by proclaiming the merits of his sparkling beverage, "colder than the mountain snow (*más fría que la nieve*)."

As the sun declines, there is again a gradual reviving, and when the vesper bell rings out his sinking knell, all nature seems to rejoice that the tyrant of the day has fallen. Now begins the bustle of enjoyment, when the citizens pour forth to breathe the evening air, and revel away the brief twilight in the walks and gardens of the Darro and Xenil.

As night closes, the capricious scene assumes new features. Light after light gradually twinkles forth; here a taper from a balconied window; there a votive lamp before the image of a saint. Thus, by degrees, the city emerges from the pervading gloom, and sparkles with scattered lights, like the starry firmament. Now break forth from court and garden, and street and lane, the tinkling of innumerable guitars, and the clicking of castanets; blending, at this lofty height, in a faint but general concert. "Enjoy the moment" is the creed of the gay and amorous Andalusian, and at no time does he practise it more zealously than on the balmy nights of summer, wooing his mistress with the dance, the love-ditty, and the passionate serenade.

WILLIAM HAZLITT

(1778–1830)

On Going a Journey

O<small>NE</small> of the pleasantest things in the world is going a journey; but I like to go by myself. I can enjoy society in a room; but out of doors, nature is company enough for me. I am then never less alone than when alone.

The fields his study, nature was his book.

I cannot see the wit of walking and talking at the same time. When I am in the country I wish to vegetate like the country. I am not for criticizing hedgerows and black cattle. I go out of town in order to forget the town and all that is in it. There are those who for this purpose go to watering-places, and carry the metropolis with them. I like more elbow-room and fewer encumbrances. I like solitude, when I give myself up to it, for the sake of solitude; nor do I ask for

a friend in my retreat,
Whom I may whisper solitude is sweet.

The soul of a journey is liberty, perfect liberty, to think, feel, do just as one pleases. We go a journey chiefly to be free of all impediments and of all inconveniences, to leave ourselves behind, much more to get rid of others. It is because I want a little breathing space to muse on indifferent matters, where Contemplation

May plume her feathers and let grow her wings,
That in the various bustle of resort
Were all too ruffled, and sometimes impair'd.

that I absent myself from the town for a while, without feeling at a loss the moment I am left by myself. Instead of a friend in a post-chaise or in a Tilbury, to exchange good things with, and vary the same stale topics over again, for once let me have a truce with impertinence. Give me the clear blue sky over my head, and the green turf beneath my feet, a winding road before me, and a three hours' march to dinner—and then to thinking!

It is hard if I cannot start some game on these lone heaths. I laugh, I run, I leap, I sing for joy. From the point of yonder rolling cloud I plunge into my past being, and revel there, as the sunburnt Indian plunges headlong into the wave that wafts him to his native shore. Then long-forgotten things, like "sunken wrack and sunless treasuries," burst upon my eager sight, and I begin to feel, think, and be myself again. Instead of an awkward silence, broken by attempts at wit or dull commonplaces, mine is that undisturbed silence of the heart which alone is perfect eloquence. No one likes puns, alliterations, antitheses, arguments, and analysis better than I do; but I sometimes had rather be without them. "Leave, oh, leave me to my repose!" I have just now other business in hand, which would seem idle to you, but is with me "very stuff o' the conscience." Is not this wild rose sweet without a comment?

Does not this daisy leap to my heart set in its coat of emerald? Yet if I were to explain to you the circumstance that has so endeared it to me, you would only smile. Had I not better then keep it to myself, and let it serve me to brood over, from here to yonder craggy point, and from thence onward to the far-distant horizon? I should be but bad company all that way, and therefore prefer being alone. I have heard it said that you may, when the moody fit comes on, walk or ride on by yourself, and indulge your reveries. But this looks like a breach of manners, a neglect of others, and you are thinking all the time that you ought to rejoin your party. "Out upon such half-faced fellow-ship," say I. I like to be either entirely to myself, or entirely at the disposal of others; to talk or be silent, to walk or sit still, to be sociable or solitary. I was pleased with an observation of Mr. Cobbett's, that "he thought it a bad French custom to drink our wine with our meals, and that an Englishman ought to do only one thing at a time." So I cannot talk and think, or indulge in melancholy musing and lively conversation by fits and starts. "Let me have a companion of my way," says Sterne, "were it but to remark how the shadows lengthen as the sun declines." It is beautifully said; but, in my opinion, this continual comparing of notes interferes with the involuntary impression of things upon the mind, and hurts the sentiment. If you only hint what you feel in a kind of dumb show, it is insipid: if you have to explain it, it is making a toil of a pleasure. You cannot read the book of nature without being perpetually put to the trouble of translating it for the benefit of others.

I am for the synthetical method on a journey in prefer-

ence to the analytical. I am content to lay in a stock of
ideas then, and to examine and anatomize them afterwards.
I want to see my vague notions float like the down of the
thistle before the breeze, and not to have them entangled
in the briars and thorns of controversy. For once, I like to
have it all my own way; and this is impossible unless you
are alone, or in such company as I do not covet. I have no
objection to argue a point with anyone for twenty miles
of measured road, but not for pleasure. If you remark the
scent of a beanfield crossing the road, perhaps your fellow-
traveller has no smell. If you point to a distant object, perhaps he is short-sighted, and has to take out his glass to
look at it.

To give way to our feelings before company seems
extravagance or affectation; and, on the other hand, to
have to unravel this mystery of our being at every turn,
and to make others take an equal interest in it (otherwise
the end is not answered), is a task to which few are com-
petent. We must "give it an understanding, but no tongue."
My old friend Coleridge, however, could do both. He
could go on in the most delightful explanatory way over
hill and dale, on a summer's day, and convert a landscape
into a didactic poem or a Pindaric ode. "He talked far
above singing." If I could so clothe my ideas in sounding
and flowing words, I might perhaps wish to have someone
with me to admire the swelling theme; or I could be more
content, were it possible for me to still hear his echoing
voice in the woods of All-Foxden. They had "that fine
madness in them which our first poets had"; and if they
could have been caught by some rare instrument, would
have breathed such strains as the following:

> *Here be woods as green*
> *As any, air likewise as fresh and sweet*
> *As when smooth Zephyrus plays on the fleet*
> *Face of the curled stream, with flow'rs as many*
> *As the young spring gives, and as choice as any;*
> *Here be all new delights, cool streams and wells*
> *Arbours o'ergrown with woodbines, caves and dells;*
> *Choose where thou wilt, whilst I sit by and sing,*
> *Or gather rushes to make many a ring*
> *For thy long fingers; tell thee tales of love,*
> *How the pale Phoebe, hunting in a grove,*
> *First saw the boy Endymion, from whose eyes*
> *She took eternal fire that never dies;*
> *How she convey'd him softly in a sleep,*
> *His temples bound with poppy, to the steep*
> *Head of old Latmos, where she stoops each night,*
> *Gilding the mountain with her brother's light,*
> *To kiss her sweetest.*

Had I words and images at command like these, I would attempt to wake the thoughts that lie slumbering on golden ridges in the evening clouds: but at the sight of nature my fancy, poor as it is, droops and closes up its leaves, like flowers at sunset. I can make nothing out on the spot: I must have time to collect myself.

I grant there is one subject on which it is pleasant to talk on a journey, and that is, what one shall have for supper when we get to our inn at night. The open air improves this sort of conversation or friendly altercation, by setting a keener edge on appetite. Every mile of the road heightens the flavour of the viands we expect at the end of it. How fine it is to enter some old town, walled and turreted, just at approach of nightfall, or to come to some straggling village, with the lights streaming through the surrounding gloom; and then, after inquiring for the best entertainment that the place affords, to "take one's ease at one's inn"! These eventful moments in our lives' history are too precious, too full of solid, heartfelt happiness to be frittered and dribbled away in imperfect sympathy. I would have them all to myself, and drain them to the last drop: they will do to talk of or to write about afterwards. What a delicate speculation it is, after drinking whole goblets of tea—

The cups that cheer, but not inebriate—

and letting the fumes ascend into the brain, to sit considering what we shall have for supper—eggs and a rasher, a rabbit smothered in onions, or an excellent veal cutlet! Sancho in such a situation once fixed on cow-heel; and his choice, though he could not help it, is not to be disparaged. Then, in the intervals of pictured scenery and Shandean contemplation, to catch the preparation and the stir in the kitchen (getting ready for the gentleman in the parlour).

These hours are sacred to silence and to musing, to be treasured up in the memory, and to feed the source of smiling thoughts hereafter. I would not waste them in idle talk; or if I must have the integrity of fancy broken in upon, I would rather it were by a stranger than a friend. A stranger takes his hue and character from the time and place; he is a part of the furniture and costume of an inn. If he is a Quaker, or from the West Riding of Yorkshire, so much the better. I do not even try to sympathize with him, and he breaks no squares. (How I love to see the camps of the gypsies, and to sigh my soul into that sort of life. If I express this feeling to another, he may qualify and spoil it with some objection.) I associate nothing with my travelling companion but present objects and passing events. In his ignorance of me and my affairs, I in a manner forget myself. But a friend reminds one of other things, rips up old grievances, and destroys the abstraction of the scene. Oh! it is great to shake off the trammels of the world and public opinion—to lose our importunate, tormenting, everlasting personal identity in the elements of nature, and become the creature of the moment, clear of all ties—to hold to the universe only by a dish of sweetbreads, and to owe nothing but the score of the evening—and no longer seeking for applause and meeting with contempt, to be known by no other title than the *gentleman in the parlour!*

There is hardly anything that shows the short-sightedness or capriciousness of the imagination more than travelling does. With change of place we change our ideas; nay, our opinions and feelings. We can by an effort indeed transport ourselves to old and long-forgotten scenes, and then the picture of the mind revives again; but we forget those that we have just left. It seems that we can think but of one place at a time. The canvas of the fancy is but of a certain extent, and if we paint one set of objects upon it, they immediately efface every other. In the country we forget the town, and in town we despise the country. "Beyond Hyde Park," says Sir Fopling Flutter, "all is a desert."

The mind can form no larger idea of space than the eye can take in at a single glance. The rest is a name written in a map, a calculation of arithmetic. For instance, what is the true signification of that immense mass of territory and population known by the name of China to us? An inch of pasteboard on a wooden globe, of no more account than a China orange! Things near us are seen of the size of life: things at a distance are diminished to the size of the understanding. We measure the universe by ourselves, and even comprehend the texture of our own being only piecemeal. In this way, however, we remember an infinity of things and places. The mind is like a mechanical instrument that plays a great variety of tunes, but it must play them in succession. One idea recalls another, but it at the same time excludes all others. In trying to renew old recollections, we cannot as it were unfold the whole web of our existence; we must pick out the single threads. So in coming to a place where we have formerly lived, and with which we have intimate associations, everyone must have found that the feeling grows more vivid the nearer we approach the spot, from the mere anticipation of the actual impression: we remember circumstances, feelings, persons, faces, names that we had not thought of for years; but for the time all the rest of the world is forgotten! To return to the question I have quitted above:

I have no objection to go to see ruins, aqueducts, pictures, in company with a friend or a party, but rather the contrary, for the former reason reversed. They are intelligible matters, and will bear talking about. The sentiment here is not tacit, but communicable and overt. Salisbury Plain is barren of criticism, but Stonehenge will bear a discussion antiquarian, picturesque, and philosophical. In setting out on a party of pleasure, the first consideration always is where we shall go to: in taking a solitary ramble, the question is what we shall meet with by the way. "The

mind is its own place"; nor are we anxious to arrive at the
end of our journey. I can myself do the honours indiffer-
ently well to works of art and curiosity. I once took a party
to Oxford with no mean *éclat*—showed them that seat of
the Muses at a distance,

With glistering spires and pinnacles adorn'd—

descanted on the learned air that breathes from the grassy
quadrangles and stone walls of halls and colleges—was at
home in the Bodleian; and at Blenheim quite superseded
the powdered cicerone that attended us, and that pointed
in vain with his wand to commonplace beauties in match-
less pictures.

As another exception to the above reasoning, I should
not feel confident in venturing on a journey in a foreign
country without a companion. I should want at intervals to
hear the sound of my own language. There is an involuntary antipathy in the mind of an Englishman to foreign
manners and notions that requires the assistance of social
sympathy to carry it off. As the distance from home in-
creases, this relief, which was at first a luxury, becomes a
passion and an appetite. A person would almost feel stifled
to find himself in the deserts of Arabia without friends and
countrymen: there must be allowed to be something in the
view of Athens or old Rome that claims the utterance of
speech; and I own that the Pyramids are too mighty for
any single contemplation. In such situations, so opposite
to all one's ordinary train of ideas, one seems a species by
one's-self, a limb torn off from society, unless one can meet
with instant fellowship and support.

Yet I did not feel this want or craving very pressing

once, when I first set my foot on the laughing shores of France. Calais was peopled with novelty and delight. The confused, busy murmur of the place was like oil and wine poured into my ears; nor did the mariners' hymn, which was sung from the top of an old crazy vessel in the harbour, as the sun went down, send an alien sound into my soul. I only breathed the air of general humanity. I walked over "the vine-covered hills and gay regions of France," erect and satisfied; for the image of man was not cast down and chained to the foot of arbitrary thrones: I was at no loss for language, for that of all the great schools of painting was open to me. The whole is vanished like a shade. Pictures, heroes, glory, freedom, all are fled: nothing remains but the Bourbons and the French people!

There is undoubtedly a sensation in travelling into foreign parts that is to be had nowhere else; but it is more pleasing at the time than lasting. It is too remote from our habitual associations to be a common topic of discourse or reference, and, like a dream or other state of existence, does not piece into our daily modes of life. It is an animated but a momentary hallucination. Those who wish to forget painful thoughts, do well to absent themselves for a while from the ties and objects that recall them; but we can be said only to fulfil our destiny in the place that gave us birth. I should on this account like well enough to spend the whole of my life in travelling abroad, if I could anywhere borrow another life to spend afterwards at home!

LOGAN PEARSALL SMITH

(1865–1946)

The Kaleidoscope

I FIND in my mind, in its miscellany of ideas and musings, a curious collection of little landscapes, shining and fading for no reason. Sometimes they are views in no way remarkable—the corner of a road, a heap of stones, an old gate. But there are many charming pictures too: as I read, between my eyes and book, the Moon washes the harvest-fields with her chill of silver; I see autumnal avenues, with the leaves falling, or swept in heaps; and storms blow among my thoughts, with the rain beating for ever on the fields. Then Winter's upward glare of snow brightens; or the pink and delicate green of Spring in the windy sunshine; or cornfields and green waters, and youths bathing in Summer's golden heat.

And as I walk about, places haunt me; a cathedral rises above a dark blue foreign town, the colour of ivory in the sunset light; now I find myself in a French garden, full of lilacs and bees, and shut-in sunshine, with the Mediterranean lounging outside its walls; now in a little college library, with busts, and the green reflected light of Oxford lawns;—and again I hear the bells, reminding me of the Oxford hours.

JAMES THURBER

(1894–   )

There's No Place Like Home

IF YOU are thinking about going abroad and want to preserve your ardor for travelling, don't pore over a little book called "Collins' Pocket Interpreters: France," which I picked up in London. Written especially to instruct the English how to speak French in the train, the hotel, the quandary, the dilemma, etc., it is, of course, equally useful —I might also say equally depressing—to Americans. I have come across a number of these helps-for-travelers, but none that has the heavy impact, the dark, cumulative power of Collins'. A writer in a London magazine, not so many years ago, mentions a phrase book got out in the era of Imperial Russia which contained this one magnificent line: "Oh dear, our postillion has been struck by lightning!" But that fantastic piece of disaster, while charming and pro- vocative—though, I daresay, quite rare even in the days of the Czars—is to Mr. Collins' modern, workaday disas- ters as Fragonard is to George Bellows, or Sarah Orne Jewett to William Faulkner. Let us turn the pages of this appalling little volume.

Each page has a list of English expressions, one under

the other, which gives them the form of verse. The French translations are run alongside. Thus, on the first page, under "The Port of Arrival," we begin (quietly enough) with "Porter, here is my baggage!"—*"Porteur, voici mes bagages!"* From then on disaster follows fast and follows faster until in the end, as you shall see, all hell breaks loose. The volume contains three times as many expressions to use when one is in trouble as when everything is going all right. This, my own experience has shown, is about the right ratio, but God spare me from some of the difficulties for which the traveler is prepared in Mr. Collins' melancholy narrative poem. I am going to leave out the French translations because, for one thing, people who get involved in the messes and tangles we are coming to invariably forget their French and scream in English, anyway. Furthermore, the French would interrupt the fine, free flow of the English and spoil what amounts to a dramatic tragedy of an overwhelming and original kind. The phrases, as I have said, run one under the other, but herein I shall have to run them one after the other (you can copy them down the other way, if you want to).

Trouble really starts in the canto called "In the Customs Shed." Here we have: "I cannot open my case." "I have lost my keys." "Help me to close this case." "I did not know that I had to pay." "I don't want to pay so much." "I cannot find my porter." "Have you seen porter 153?" That last query is a little master stroke of writing, I think, for in those few words we have a graphic picture of a tourist lost in a jumble of thousands of bags and scores of customs men, looking frantically for one of at least a hundred and fifty-three porters. We feel that the tourist will not find porter 153, and the note of frustration has been struck.

Our tourist (accompanied by his wife, I like to think) finally gets on the train for Paris—having lost his keys and not having found his porter—and it comes time presently to go to the dining car, although he probably has no appetite, for the customs men, of course, have had to break open that one suitcase. Now, I think, it is the wife who begins to crumble: "Someone has taken my seat." "Excuse me, sir, that seat is mine." "I cannot find my ticket!" "I have left my ticket in the compartment." "I will go and look for it." "I have left my gloves (my purse) in the dining car." Here the note of frenzied disintegration so familiar to all travelers abroad, is sounded. Next comes "The Sleeper," which begins, ominously, with "What is the matter?" and ends with "May I open the window?" "Can you open this window, please?" We realize, of course, that *nobody* is going to be able to open the window and that the tourist and his wife will suffocate. In this condition they arrive in Paris, and the scene there, on the crowded station platform, is done with superb economy of line: "I have left something in the train." "A parcel, an overcoat." "A mackintosh, a stick." "An umbrella, a camera." "A fur, a suitcase." The travelers have now begun to go completely to pieces, in the grand manner.

Next comes an effective little interlude about an airplane trip, which is one of my favorite passages in this swift and sorrowful tragedy: "I want to reserve a place in the plane leaving tomorrow morning." "When do we start?" "Can we get anything to eat on board?" "When do we arrive?" "I feel sick." "Have you any paper bags for air-sickness?" "The noise is terrible." "Have you any cotton wool?" "When are we going to land?" This brief masterpiece caused me to cancel an air trip from London to Paris and go the easy way, across the Channel.

We now come to a section called "At the Hotel," in which things go from worse to awful: "Did you not get my letter?" "I wrote to you three weeks ago." "I asked for a first-floor room." "If you can't give me something better, I shall go away." "The chambermaid never comes when I ring." "I cannot sleep at night, there is so much noise." "I have just had a wire. I must leave at once." Panic has begun to set in, and it is not appeased any by the advent of "The Chambermaid": "Are you the chambermaid?" "There are no towels here." "The sheets on this bed are damp." "This room is not clean." "I have seen a mouse in the room." "You will have to set a mouse trap here." (I am sure all you brave people who are still determined to come to France will want to know how to say "mouse trap" in French: it's *souricière;* but you better bring one with you.) The bells of hell at this point begin to ring in earnest: "These shoes are not mine." "I put my shoes here, where are they now?" "The light is not good." "The bulb is broken." "The radiator is too warm." "The radiator doesn't work." "It is cold in this room." "This is not clean, bring me another." "I don't like this." "I can't eat this. Take it away!"

I somehow now see the tourist's wife stalking angrily out of the hotel, to get away from it all (without any shoes on), and, properly enough, the booklet seems to follow

her course—first under "Guides and Interpreters": "You
are asking too much." "I will not give you any more." "I
shall call a policeman." "He can settle this affair." Then
under "Inquiring the Way": "I am lost." "I was looking
for ————." "Someone robbed me." "That man robbed
me." "That man is following me everywhere." She rushes
to "The Hairdresser," where, for a change, everything
goes quite smoothly until: "The water is too hot, you are
scalding me!" Then she goes shopping, but there is no sur-
cease: "You have not given me the right change." "I
bought this two days ago." "It doesn't work." "It is
broken." "It is torn." "It doesn't fit me." Then to a restau-
rant for a snack and a reviving cup of tea: "This is not
fresh." "This piece is too fat." "This doesn't smell very
nice." "There is a mistake in the bill." "While I was dining
someone has taken my purse." "I have left my glasses (my
watch) (a ring) in the lavatory." Madness has now come
upon her and she rushes wildly out into the street. Her
husband, I think, has at the same time plunged blindly out
of the hotel to find her. We come then, quite naturally, to
"Accident," which is calculated to keep the faint of heart
—nay, the heart of oak—safely at home by his own fireside: "There has been an accident!" "Go and fetch a policeman quickly." "Is there a doctor near here?" "Send for
the ambulance." "He is seriously injured." "She has been
run over." "He has been knocked down." "Someone has
fallen in the water." "The ankle, the arm." "The back, a
bone." "The face, the finger." "The foot, the head." "The
knee, the leg." "The neck, the nose." "The wrist, the shoulder." "He has broken his arm." "He has broken his leg."

"He has a sprained ankle." "He has a sprained wrist." "He is losing blood." "He has fainted." "He has lost consciousness." "He has burnt his face." "It is swollen." "It is bleeding." "Bring some cold water." "Help me to carry him." (Apparently, you just let *her* lie there, while you attend to him—but, of course, she was merely run over, whereas he has taken a terrific tossing around.)

We next see the husband and wife back in their room at the dreary hotel, both in bed, and both obviously hysterical. This scene is entitled "Illness": "I am feeling very ill, send for the doctor." "I have pains in ———." "I have pains all over." "The back, the chest." "The ear, the head." "The eyes, the heart." "The joints, the kidneys." "The lungs, the stomach." "The throat, the tongue." "Put out your tongue." "The heart is affected." "I feel a pain here." "He is not sleeping well." "He cannot eat." "My stomach is out of order." "She is feverish." "I have caught a cold." "I have caught a chill." "He has a temperature." "I have a cough." "Will you give me a prescription?" "What must I do?" "Must I stay in bed?" "I feel better." "When will you come and see me again?" "Biliousness, rheumatism." "Insomnia, sunstroke." "Fainting, a fit." "Hoarseness, sore throat." "The medicine, the remedy." "A poultice, a draught." "A tablespoonful, a teaspoonful." "A sticking plaster, senna." "Iodine." That last suicidal bleat for iodine is, to me, a masterful touch.

Our couple finally get on their feet again, for travelers are tough—they've got to be—but we see under the next heading, "Common Words and Phrases," that they are left forever punch-drunk and shattered: "Can I help you?"

"Excuse me." "Carry on!" "Look here!" "Look down there!" "Look up there!" "Why, how?" "When, where?" "Because." "That's it!" "It is too much, it is too dear." "It is very cheap." "Who, what, which?" "Look out!" Those are Valkyries, one feels, riding around, and above, and under our unhappy husband and wife. The book sweeps on to a mad operatic ending of the tragedy, with all the strings and brasses and woodwinds going full blast: "Where are we going?" "Where are you going?" "Come quickly and see!" "I shall call a policeman." "Bring a policeman!" "I shall stay here." "Will you help me?" "Help! Fire!" "Who are you?" "I don't know you." "I don't want to speak to you." "Leave me alone." "That will do." "You are mistaken." "It was not I." "I didn't do it." "I will give you nothing." "Go away now!" "It has nothing to do with me." "Where should one apply?" "What must I do?" "What have I done?" "I have done nothing." "I have already paid you." "I have paid you enough." "Let me pass!" "Where is the British consulate?" The oboes take that last, despairing wail, and the curtain comes down.

So you're going to France?

✳ PART IV ✳

THIS AND THAT

LEIGH HUNT

(1784–1859)

Getting Up on Cold Mornings

AN ITALIAN author—Giulio Cordara, a Jesuit—has written a poem upon insects, which he begins by insisting, that those troublesome and abominable little animals were created for our annoyance, and that they were certainly not inhabitants of Paradise. We of the north may dispute this piece of theology; but on the other hand, it is clear as the snow on the house-tops, that Adam was not under the necessity of shaving; and that when Eve walked out of her delicious bower, she did not step upon ice three inches thick.

Some people say it is a very easy thing to get up of a cold morning. You have only, they tell you, to take the resolution; and the thing is done. This may be very true; just as a boy at school has only to take a flogging, and the thing is over. But we have not at all made up our minds upon it; and we find it a very pleasant exercise to discuss the matter, candidly, before we get up. This at least is not idling, though it may be lying. In the first place, says the injured but calm appealer, I have been warm all night, and find my system in a state perfectly suitable to a warm-blooded ani-

mal. To get out of this state into the cold, besides the in-
harmonious and uncritical abruptness of the transition, is
so unnatural to such a creature, that the poets, refining
upon the tortures of the damned, make one of their greatest
agonies consist in being suddenly transported from heat to
cold,—from fire to ice. They are "haled" out of their
"beds," says Milton, by "harpy-footed furies,"—fellows
who come to call them. On my first movement towards the
anticipation of getting up, I find that such parts of the
sheets and bolster, as are exposed to the air of the room, are
stone-cold. On opening my eyes, the first thing that meets
them is my own breath rolling forth, as if in the open air,
like smoke out of a cottage chimney. Think of this symp-
tom. Then I turn my eyes sideways and see the window
all frozen over. Think of that. Then the servant comes in.
"It is very cold this morning, is it not?" "Very cold,
Sir." "Very cold indeed, isn't it?" "Very cold indeed, Sir."
"More than usually so, isn't it, even for this weather?"
(Here the servant's wit and good-nature are put to a considerable test, and the inquirer lies on thorns for the an-
swer.) "Why, Sir . . . I think it *is*." (Good creature!
There is not a better, or more truth-telling servant going.)
"I must rise, however—get me some warm water." Here
comes a fine interval between the departure of the servant
and the arrival of the hot water; during which, of course,
it is of "no use" to get up. The hot water comes.
"Is it quite hot?" "Yes, Sir." "Perhaps too hot for shaving; I must wait a little?" "No, Sir; it will just do." (There
is an over-nice propriety sometimes, an officious zeal of
virtue, a little troublesome.) "Oh—the shirt—you must

air my clean shirt; linen gets very damp this weather."
"Yes, Sir." Here another delicious five minutes. A knock
at the door. "Oh, the shirt—very well. My stockings—I
think the stockings had better be aired too." "Very well,
Sir." Here another interval. At length everything is ready,
except myself.

Thomson the poet, who exclaims in his *Seasons*—

Falsely luxurious! Will not man awake?

used to lie in bed till noon, because he said he had no motive
in getting up. He could imagine the good of rising; but
then he could also imagine the good of lying still; and his
exclamation, it must be allowed, was made upon summer-
time, not winter. We must proportion the argument to the
individual character. A money-getter may be drawn out of
his bed by three and four pence; but this will not suffice for
a student. A proud man may say, "What shall I think of
myself, if I don't get up?" but the more humble one will be
content to waive his prodigious notion of himself, out of
respect to his kindly bed. The mechanical man shall get up
without any ado at all; and so shall the barometer.

An ingenious lier in bed will find hard matter of discussion even on the score of health and longevity. He will ask
us for our proofs and precedents of the ill effects of lying
later in cold weather; and sophisticate much on the advantages of an even temperature of body; of the natural propensity (pretty universal) to have one's way; and of the
animals that roll themselves up, and sleep all the winter. As
to longevity, he will ask whether the longest life is of necessity the best; and whether Holborn is the handsomest
street in London.

We only know of one confounding, not to say confounded argument, fit to overturn the huge luxury, the "enormous bliss"—of the vice in question. The best way to deal with him is this, especially for a lady; for we earnestly recommend the use of that sex on such occasions, if not somewhat *over*-persuasive; since extremes have an awkward knack of meeting. First then, admit all the ingeniousness of what he says, telling him that the bar has been deprived of an excellent lawyer. Then look at him in the most good-natured manner in the world, with a mixture of assent and appeal in your countenance, and tell him that you are waiting breakfast for him; that you never like to breakfast without him; that you really want it too; that the servants want theirs; that you shall not know how to get the house into order, unless he rises; and that you are sure he would do things twenty times worse, even than getting out of his warm bed, to put them all into good humour and a state of comfort.

Other little helps of appeal may be thrown in, as occasion requires. You may tell a lover, for instance, that lying in bed makes people corpulent; a father, that you wish him to complete the fine manly example he sets his children; a lady, that she will injure her bloom or her shape, which M. or W. admires so much; and a student or artist, that he is always so glad to have done a good day's work, in his best manner.

READER. And pray, Mr. Indicator, how do *you* behave yourself in this respect?

INDIC. Oh, Madam, perfectly, of course; like all advisers.

READER. Nay, I allow that your mode of argument does not look quite so suspicious as the old way of sermonizing and severity, but I have my doubts, especially from that laugh of yours. If I should look in tomorrow morning—

INDIC. Ah, Madam, the look in of a face like yours does anything with me. It shall fetch me up at nine, if you please —*six*, I meant to say.

ROBERT LOUIS STEVENSON

(1850–1894)

El Dorado

It seems as if a great deal were attainable in a world
where there are so many marriages and decisive battles,
and where we all, at certain hours of the day, and with
great gusto and dispatch stow a portion of victuals finally
and irretrievably into the bag which contains us. And it
would seem also, on a hasty view, that the attainment of as
much as possible was the one goal of man's contentious life.
And yet, as regards the spirit, this is but a semblance. We
live in an ascending scale when we live happily, one thing
leading to another in an endless series. There is always a
new horizon for onward-looking men, and although we
dwell on a small planet, immersed in petty business and not
enduring beyond a brief period of years, we are so consti-
tuted that our hopes are inaccessible, like stars, and the
term of hoping is prolonged until the term of life.

To be truly happy is a question of how we begin and
not of how we end, of what we want and not of what we
have. An aspiration is a joy forever, a possession as solid as
a landed estate, a fortune which we can never exhaust and
which gives us year by year a revenue of pleasurable ac-

tivity. To have many of these is to be spiritually rich. Life is only a very dull and ill-directed theater unless we have some interests in the piece; and to those who have neither art nor science, the world is a mere arrangement of colors, or a rough footway where they may very well break their shins.

It is in virtue of his own desires and curiosities that any man continues to exist with even patience, that he is charmed by the look of things and people, and that he wakens every morning with a renewed appetite for work and pleasure. Desire and curiosity are the two eyes through which he sees the world in the most enchanted colors: it is they that make women beautiful or fossils interesting: and the man may squander his estate and come to beggary, but if he keeps these two amulets he is still rich in the possibilities of pleasure. Suppose he could take one meal so compact and comprehensive that he should never hunger any more; suppose him, at a glance, to take in all the features of the world and allay the desire for knowledge; suppose him to do the like in any province of experience—would not that man be in a poor way for amusement ever after?

One who goes touring on foot with a single volume in his knapsack reads with circumspection, pausing often to reflect, and often laying the book down to contemplate the landscape or the prints in the inn parlor; for he fears to come to an end of his entertainment, and be left companionless on the last stages of his journey. A young fellow recently finished the works of Thomas Carlyle, winding up, if we remember aright, with the ten note-books upon Frederick the Great. "What!" cried the young fellow, in consternation, "is there no more Carlyle? Am I left to the daily papers?" A more celebrated instance is that of Alexander, who wept bitterly because he had no more worlds to subdue. And when Gibbon had finished the *Decline and Fall*, he had only a few moments of joy; and it was with a "sober melancholy" that he parted from his labors.

Happily we all shoot at the moon with ineffectual arrows; our hopes are set on inaccessible El Dorado; we come to an end of nothing here below. Interests are only plucked up to sow themselves again, like mustard. You would think, when the child was born, there would be an end to trouble; and yet it is only the beginning of fresh anxieties; and when you have seen it through its teething and its education, and at last its marriage, alas! it is only to have new fears, new quivering sensibilities, with every day; and the health of your children's children grows as touching a concern as that of your own.

Again, when you have married your wife, you would think you were got upon a hilltop, and might begin to go downward by an easy slope. But you have only ended courting to begin marriage. Falling in love and winning love are often difficult tasks to overbearing and rebellious spirits; but to keep in love is also a business of some importance, to which both man and wife must bring kindness and good-will. The true love story commences at the altar, when there lies before the married pair a most beautiful contest of wisdom and generosity, and a life-long struggle towards an unattainable ideal. Unattainable? Ay, surely unattainable, from the very fact that they are two instead of one.

"Of making books there is no end," complained the Preacher; and did not perceive how highly he was praising letters as an occupation. There is no end, indeed, to making books or experiments, or to travel, or to gathering wealth. Problem gives rise to problem. We may study forever, and we are never as learned as we would. We have never made a statue worthy of our dreams. And when we have discovered a continent, or crossed a chain of mountains, it is only to find another ocean or another plain upon the further side. In the infinite universe there is room for our swiftest diligence and to spare. It is not like the works of Carlyle, which can be read to an end. Even in a corner of it, in a private park, or in the neighborhood of a single hamlet, the weather and the seasons keep so deftly changing that although we walk there for a lifetime there will be always something new to startle and delight us.

There is only one wish realizable on the earth; only one thing that can be perfectly attained: Death. And from a variety of circumstances we have no one to tell us whether it be worth attaining.

A strange picture we make on our way to our chimaeras, ceaselessly marching, grudging ourselves the time for rest; indefatigable, adventurous pioneers. It is true that we shall never reach the goal; it is even more than probable that there is no such place; and if we lived for centuries and were endowed with the powers of a god, we should find ourselves not much nearer what we wanted at the end. O toiling hands of mortals! O unwearied feet, travelling ye know not whither! Soon, soon, it seems to you, you must come forth on some conspicuous hilltop, and but a little way further, against the setting sun, descry the spires of El Dorado. Little do ye know your own blessedness; for to travel hopefully is a better thing than to arrive, and the true success is to labor.

E. V. LUCAS

(1868–1938)

The Town Week

Iᴛ ɪs odd that "Mondayish" is the only word which the
days of the week have given us; since Monday is not alone
in possessing a positive and peculiar character. Why not
"Tuesdayish" or "Wednesdayish"? Each word would
convey as much meaning to me, "Tuesdayish" in particular, for Monday's cardinal and reprehensible error of
beginning the business week seems to me almost a virtue
compared with Tuesday's utter flatness. To begin a new
week is no fault at all, though tradition has branded it as
one. To begin is a noble accomplishment; but to continue
dully, to be the tame follower of a courageous beginner, to
be the second day in a week of action, as in Tuesday's case
—that is deplorable, if you like.

Monday can be flat enough, but in a different way from
Tuesday. Monday is flat because one has been idling, perhaps unconsciously absorbing notions of living like the
lilies; because so many days must pass before the week
ends; because yesterday is no more. But Tuesday has the
sheer essential flatness of nonentity; Tuesday is nothing.
If you would know how absolutely nothing it is, go to a

week-end hotel at, say Brighton, and stay on after the Saturday-to-Monday population has flitted. On Tuesday you touch the depths. So does the menu—no *chef* ever exerted himself for a Tuesday guest. Tuesday is also very difficult to spell, many otherwise cultured ladies putting the *e* before the *u:* and why not? What right has Tuesday to any preference?

With all its faults, Monday has a positive character. Monday brings a feeling of revolt; Tuesday, the base craven, reconciles us to the machine. I am not surprised that the recent American revivalists held no meetings on Mondays. It was a mark of their astuteness; they knew that the wear and tear of overcoming the Monday feeling of the greater part of their audience would exhaust them before their magnetism began to have play; while a similarly stubborn difficulty would confront them in the remaining portion sunk in apathy by the thought that tomorrow would be Tuesday. It is this presage of certain tedium which has robbed Monday evening of its "glittering star." Yet since nothing so becomes a flat day as the death of it, Tuesday evening's glittering star (it is Wordsworth's phrase) is of the brightest—for is not the dreary day nearly done, and is not tomorrow Wednesday the bland?

With Wednesday, the week stirs itself, turns over, begins to wake. There are matinees on Wednesday; on Wednesdays some of the more genial weekly papers come out. The very word has a good honest round air—Wednesday. Things, adventures, might happen very naturally on Wednesday; but that nothing ever happened on a Tuesday

I am convinced. In summer Wednesday has often close finishes at Lord's, and it is a day on which one's friends are pretty sure to be accessible. On Monday they may not have returned from the country; on Friday they have begun to go out of town again; but on Wednesday they are here, at home—are solid. I am sure it is my favorite day.

(Even politicians, so slow as a rule to recognize the kindlier, more generous, side of life, realized for many years that Wednesday was a day on which they had no right to conduct their acrimonious business for more than an hour or so. Much of the failure of the last Government may be traced to their atheistical decision no longer to remember Wednesday to keep it holy.)

On Thursday the week falls back a little; the stirring of Wednesday is forgotten; there is a return to the folding of the hands. I am not sure that Thursday has not become the real day of rest. That it is a good honest day is the most that can be said for it. It is certainly not Thor's day any longer —if my reading of the character of the blacksmith-god is true. There is nothing strong and downright and fine about it. Compared with Tuesday's small beer, Thursday is almost champagne; but none the less they are related. One can group them together. If I were a business man, I should, I am certain, sell my shares at a loss on Monday and at a profit on Wednesday and Friday, but on Tuesday and Thursday I should get for them exactly what I gave.

I group Friday with Wednesday as a day that can be friendly to me, but it has not Wednesday's quality. Wednesday is calm, assured, urbane; Friday allows itself to be a little flurried and excited. Wednesday stands alone;

Friday to some extent throws in its lot with Saturday. Friday is too busy. Too many papers come out, too many bags are packed, on Friday. But herein, of course, is some of its virtue; it is the beginning of the end, the forerunner of Saturday and Sunday. If anticipation, as the moralists say, is better than the realization, Friday is perhaps the best day of the week, for one spends much of it in thinking of the morrow and what of good it should bring forth. Friday's greatest merit is perhaps that it paves the way to Saturday and the cessation of work. That it ever was really unlucky I greatly doubt.

And so we come to Saturday and Sunday. But here the analyst falters, for Saturday and Sunday pass from the region of definable days. Monday and Tuesday, Wednesday and Thursday and Friday, these are days with a character fixed more or less for all. But Saturday and Sunday are what we individually make of them. In one family they are friends, associates; in another as ill-assorted as Socrates and Xantippe. For most of us Saturday is not exactly a day at all, it is a collection of hours, part work, part pleasure, and all restlessness. It is a day that we plan for, and therefore it is often a failure. I have no distinct and unvarying impression of Saturday, except that trains are full and late and shops shut too early.

Sunday even more than Saturday is different as people are different. To the godly it is a day of low tones, its minutes go by muffled; to the children of the godly it is eternity. To the ungodly it is a day jeopardized by an interest in barometers that is almost too poignant. To one man it is an interruption of the week; to another it is the week itself, and all the rest of the days are but preparations for it. One cannot analyse Saturday and Sunday.

But Monday? There we are on solid ground again. Monday—but I have discussed Monday already: that is one of its principal characteristics, that it is always coming round again, pretending to be new. It is always the same in reality.

E. B. WHITE

(1899–   )

Memorandum

Today I should carry the pumpkins and squash from
the back porch to the attic. The nights are too frosty to
leave them outdoors any longer. And as long as I am making some trips to the attic I should also take up the boat
cushions and the charts and the stuff from the galley and
also a fishing rod that belongs up in the attic. Today I
should finish filling in the trench we dug for the water pipe
and should haul two loads of beach gravel from the Nas-
keag bar to spread on top of the clay fill. And I should stop
in and pay the Reverend Mr. Smith for the gravel I got a
month or two ago and ask him if he has seen a bear.

I ought to finish husking the corn and wheel the old
stalks out and dump them on the compost pile, and while I
am out there I should take a fork and pitch over the weeds
that were thrown at the edge of the field last August and
rake the little windfalls from under the apple tree and
pitch them on to the heap too. I ought to go down to the
shore at dead low water and hook on to the mooring with
a chain and make the chain fast to the float, so that the tide
will pick up the mooring rock and I can tow the whole

thing ashore six hours later. I ought to knock the wedges out from the frames of the pier, put a line on the frames, and tow them in on the high water. First, though, I would have to find a line long enough to tie every frame. If I'm to do any work at the shore I ought first put a cement patch on the leak in my right boot. After the frames are on the beach another fellow and myself ought to carry them up and stack them. And there is probably enough rockweed on the beach now, so that I ought to bring up a load or two for the sheep shed. I ought to find out who it is that is shooting coot down in the cove today, just to satisfy my own curiosity. He was out before daybreak with his decoys, but I do not think he has got any birds.

I ought to take up the wire fence round the chicken range today, roll it up in bundles, tie them with six-thread, and store them at the edge of the woods. Then I ought to move the range houses off the field and into the corner of the woods and set them up on blocks for the winter, but I ought to sweep them out first and clean the roosts with a wire brush. It would be a good idea to have a putty knife in my pocket, for scraping. I ought to add a bag of phosphate to the piles of hen dressing that have accumulated under the range houses and spread the mixture on the field, to get it ready for plowing. And I ought to decide whether to plow just the range itself or to turn over a little more on the eastern end. On my way in from the range I ought to stop at the henhouse long enough to climb up and saw off an overhanging branch from the apple tree—it might tear the paper roof in the first big wind storm. I shall have to get a ladder, of course, and a saw.

Today I certainly ought to go over to the mill and get four twelve-inch boards, twelve feet long and half an inch thick, to use in building three new hoppers for dry mash feeding to my pullets, which are now laying seventy-eight per cent and giving me about eighty dozen eggs a week. I should also need one board which would be an inch thick, for the end pieces and for making the ends of the reels. I shouldn't need anything for the stands because I have enough stuff round the place to build the stands—which I had better make twenty-three inches high from floor to perch. If I were to make them less than that, the birds on the floor would pick at the vents of the birds feeding.

I ought to get some shingle nails and some spikes while I am at it, as we are out of those things. And I ought to sharpen the blade of my plane if I am going to build some hoppers. I ought to take the cutting-off saw and have it filed, as long as I am going over to the mill anyway. On the way back I ought to stop in at Frank Hamilton's house and put in my application for government lime and super, because I shall be passing his house and might just as well take advantage of it. Frank will ask me to sit down and talk a while, I imagine.

It is high time I raked up the bayberry brush which has been lying in the pasture since the August mowing. This would be a good chance to burn it today because we have had a rain and it is safe to burn. But before burning it I ought to find out whether it is really better for the pasture to burn stuff like that or to let it rot for dressing. I suppose there is so much wood in it, it wouldn't rot up quickly and should be burned. Besides, I was once told in high-school chemistry that no energy is ever lost to the world, and presumably the ashes from the fires will strengthen my pasture in their own way.

I ought to take the buck lamb out of the flocks of lambs today, before he gets to work on the ewe lambs, because I don't want them to get bred. I don't know just where to put him, but I ought to decide that today, and put him there. I should send away today for some phenothiazine so that I can drench my sheep next week. It would probably be a good idea to try phenothiazine this time, instead of copper sulphate, which just gets the stomach worms and doesn't touch the nodular worms or the large-mouth bowel worms. And I ought to close the big doors on the north side of the barn cellar and board them up and bank them, so that the place won't be draughty down there at night when the sheep come in, as they are beginning to do. I have been thinking I ought to enlarge the south door so that I won't lose any lambs next spring from the ewes jamming through the narrow single opening, and this would be the time to do that.

Today I ought to start rebuilding the racks in the sheep shed, to fix them so the sheep can't pull hay out and waste it. There is a way to do this, and I know the way. So I am all set. Also I ought to fix up the pigpen down there in the barn cellar too and sweeten it up with a coat of whitening, so that I can get the pig indoors, because the nights are pretty cold now. The trough will probably not have to be rebuilt this year because last year I put a zinc binding all around the edges of it. (But if I *shouldn't* get round to fixing up the pen I should at least carry a forkful of straw down to the house where the pig now is—I should at least do that.)

This would be a good day to put in a new light in the window in the woodshed, and also there is one broken in the shop and one in the henhouse, so the sensible thing would be to do them all at once, as long as I have the putty all worked up and the glass cutter out. I ought to hook up the stove in the shop today, and get it ready for winter use. And I ought to run up the road and see Bert and find out why he hasn't delivered the cord of slab-wood he said he was going to bring me. At any rate, I ought to make a place in the cellar for it today, which will mean cleaning house down there a little and neating up, and finding a better place to keep my flats and fillers for my egg cases. Incidentally, I ought to collect eggs right now, so there won't be any breakage in the nests.

It just occurred to me that if I'm going to the mill today I ought to measure the truck and figure out what I shall need in the way of hardwood boards to build a set of sideboards and a headboard and a tailboard for my stakes. I ought to bring these boards back with me along with the pine for the hoppers. I shall need two bolts for the ends of each sideboard, and one bolt for the cleat in the middle, and two bolts for the ends of each of the head- and tailboards, and there will be three each of them, so that makes fifty-four bolts I shall need, and the stakes are about an inch and a half through and the boards will be three-quarters, so that makes two inches and a quarter, and allow another half inch for washer and nut. About a three-inch bolt would do it. I better get them today.

Another thing I ought to do is take that grass seed that the mice have been getting into in the barn and store it in a wash boiler or some pails or something. I ought to set some mousetraps tonight, I mustn't forget. I ought to set one upstairs, I guess, in the little northeast chamber where the pipe comes through from the set tubs in the back kitchen, because this is the Mouse Fifth Avenue, and it would be a good chance for a kill. I ought to gather together some old clothes and stuff for the rummage sale to raise money to buy books for the town library, and I ought to rake the barnyard and wheel the dressing down into the barn cellar where it will be out of the weather, because there is a lot of good dressing there right now. I ought to note down on the calendar in my room that I saw the ewe named Galbreath go to buck day before yesterday, so I can have her lambing date. Hers will be the first lamb next spring, and it will be twins because she is a twinner. Which reminds me I ought to write Mike Galbreath a letter. I have been owing him one since before Roosevelt was elected for the third term. I certainly should do that, it has been such a long time. I should do it today while it is in my mind.

One thing I ought to do today is to take a small Stillson wrench and go down cellar and tighten the packing nut on the water pump so it won't drip. I could do that when I am down there making a place for the slabwood—it would save steps to combine the two things. I also ought to stir the litter in the henpen in the barn where the Barred Rocks are, and in the henhouse where the crossbred birds are; and then fill some bushel baskets with shavings and add them to the litter in the places where it needs deepening. The dropping boards under the broody coops need cleaning and I should do that at the same time, since I will be out there anyway. As far as litter is concerned, a man could take and rake the lawn under the maples where there is such an accumulation of leaves and add these dry leaves to the litter in the houses for the birds to scratch around in. Anything to keep their minds occupied in healthy channels.

Today I intend to pull the young alders in the field on the north side, as they are beginning to get ahead of me. I must do that today, probably later on this afternoon. A bush hook would be a good tool for that. I should also clean up the remaining garden trash and add it to the compost, saving out whatever the sheep might eat, and should remove the pipe from the well under the apple tree and store it down below in the barn.

I also think I had better call up a buyer and get rid of my ten old hens, since we have canned all we are going to need. After the hens are gone I shall no longer need the borrowed range house that they are living in and I can get two long poles, lash them on behind the truck, and load the house on and drag it up to flatten the ends of the poles so they won't dig into the highway, although the tar is so cold now they probably wouldn't dig in much anyway. Still, the thing to do is do it right.

Another thing I should try to manage to do today is to earmark the two pure-bred lambs. That will be easy enough—it just means finding the ear tags that I put away in a drawer or some place last spring and finding the special pliers that you have to use in squeezing a tag into a sheep's ear. I think I know where those pliers are, I think they are right in my cabinet next to that jar of rubber cement. I shall have to get the lambs up, but they will come without much trouble now because they are hungry. I *could* take the buck away at the same time if I could think of a place to put him.

Today I want to get word to Walter about the plowing of the garden pieces, and I had also better arrange down cellar about a bin for the roots, because on account of the extra amount of potatoes we have it will mean a little re-arranging down there in order to get everything in. But I can do that when I am down tightening the nut on the pump. I ought to take the car into the village today to get an inspection sticker put on it; however, on second thought if I am going to the mill I guess it would be better to go in the truck and have a sticker put on *that* while I am seeing about the lumber, and then I can bring the boards back with me. But I mustn't be away at low water otherwise I won't be able to hook on to the mooring.

Tomorrow is Tuesday and the egg truck will be coming through in the morning to pick up my cases, so I must finish grading and packing the eggs today—I have about fifty dozen packed and only ten to go to make up the two cases. Then I must nail up the cases and make out the tags and tack them on, and lug the cases over to the cellar door, ready to be taken out in the morning, as the expressman is apt to get here early. I've also got to write a letter today to a publisher who wrote me asking what happened to the book manuscript I was supposed to turn in a year ago last spring, and I also should take the green chair in the living room to Eliot Sweet so that he can put in some little buttons that keep coming out all the time. I can throw the chair into the truck and drop it by his shop on my way to town. If I am going to take the squashes and pumpkins up to the attic I had better take the old blankets which we have been covering them with nights, and hang them on the line to dry. I also ought to nail a pole up somewhere in the barn to hang grain sacks on so the rats won't be able to get at them and gnaw holes in them; empty sacks are worth ten cents for the heavy ones and five cents for the cotton ones, and they mount up quite fast and run into money. I mustn't forget to do that today—it won't take but a minute.

I've got to see about getting a birthday present for my wife today, but I can't think of anything. Her birthday is past anyway. There were things going on here at the time and I didn't get around to getting her a present but I haven't forgotten about it. Possibly when I am in the village I can find something.

If I'm going to rebuild the racks for the sheep it would be a good idea to have the mill rip out a lot of two-inch slats for me while I am there, as I shall need some stuff like that. I ought to make a list, I guess. And I mustn't forget shingle nails and the spikes. There is a place on the bottom step of the stairs going down into the woodshed where the crocus sack which I nailed on to the step as a foot-wiper is torn off, and somebody might catch his foot in that and take a fall. I certainly should fix that today before someone has a nasty fall. The best thing would be to rip the old sack off and tack a new one on. A man should have some roofing nails if he is going to make a neat job of tacking a sack on to a step. I think I may have some but I'd better look. I can look when I go out to get the Stillson wrench that I shall need when I go down to tighten the packing nut on the pump, and if I haven't any I can get some when I go to town.

I've been spending a lot of time here typing, and I see it is four o'clock already and almost dark, so I had better get going. Specially since I ought to get a haircut while I am at it.

CLIFTON FADIMAN

(1904–   )

Fadiman's Law of Optimum Improvement

Two scrambled eggs was what I ordered from the pleasant-faced drug-store counterman.

"On buttered toast," he declared firmly. "White, rye, gluten, marmalade or jam."

"Just two scrambled eggs," I muttered.

He eyed me with suspicion. A pause. Then, "Potatoes on the side," he stated.

"Just two scrambled eggs."

Another pause. "Nothing on the side?"

Down but still twitching, I said, "Eggs."

"Coffee now or later?"

"No coffee. Eggs."

Lost in misgivings, he prepared the eggs and was about to crown them with a generous bouquet of parsley, when I quavered, "Just the eggs—no parsley."

The eggs were fine. Asking for salt and pepper helped to patch things up a little, but I know I left the counter under a cloud.

Man, boy, and Master of Ceremonies, I have worked in

radio and television for over fifteen years. During this period—such is the public's good sense—I have drawn weighable fan mail only once. That was when, through the courtesy of an obliging network, I explained the difficulty I had always met in getting a ham sandwich. By a ham sandwich I meant a ham sandwich—a slice of ham between two pieces of buttered bread, minus lettuce, parsley, olives, pickles, carrots, shredded cabbage, mayonnaise, whipped cream. My open confession attracted many heartfelt letters, all from males.

"Man wants but little here below," the poet Goldsmith tells us. But try to get it. Try to get potatoes without parsley. A Martini without the olive. An Old-Fashioned or an ice-cream sundae without the cherry. Soft-collar shirts laundered without starch in the collar. A jacket pressed without creases in the sleeves. A cigarette box without a horse's head on it. A bottle of pills without an almost unremovable wad of cotton below the stopper. Cocktail napkins without floral curlicues. A baby's crib in a solid color (not pink or blue) without cherubs or roses stamped on the headboard.

Try, just try, to pay a bill without going through a forest of Stuffers and Fillers. The other day I opened an envelope from a New York department store with which my wife is at present conducting a fervent romance. After seventeen minutes passed in investigating the contents of the envelope, I succeeded in unearthing a bill for $17.60.

You may well ask why it took seventeen minutes to find the bill. I may well tell you. Along with the bill were eleven enclosures of varying sizes. They were all beautifully written and expensively illustrated, these stuffers were; and, if I only had had the time or were in jail or quarantine, I could have spent an exciting hour and a half reading them.

One pleaded with me to buy the latest patent moth-killer. Another directed my attention to bras in heavenly tissue-skin nylon. Another offered me my very own printed airmail stationery. Another pressed upon me the virtues of an electric shoeshine boy (AC only). Another made it clear that life was dust and ashes without a Koolfoam airy cellular latex pillow. Another urged an automatic snoozing chair. Still another tantalized me with the possibility of owning a complete flower master-kit, containing more than a hundred items for arranging flowers.

A man who gets a bill wants to be able to remove it at once from its envelope and either pay it or invent some excuse for not paying it. He does not want to receive at the same time a complete inventory of the store's merchandise. Three times out of four it is virtually impossible to find the bill without the help of two secretaries. By the time it is found the debtor is bewildered to the point of fury.

In our kitchen we have a garbage-can. A pedal is attached to its base. As you step on the pedal, the lid flies up, you throw in the disposables with one hand, the other hand being completely free to play the piano. That's the theory. In practice the foot slips off the pedal and you find yourself guiltily lifting the lid with your crude bare hands. Or it partially slips off the pedal and the lid opens shyly, just wide enough to admit a postcard. Or it works perfectly, but, the can being empty, the lid bangs up with enough power to send the entire contraption skidding along the floor, and enough clatter to wake up the dramatic critics at the first night of an Ibsen revival.

A bottle of ink used to be a bottle of ink. You filled your pen by dipping it into the bottle. Today my ink bottle comes equipped with a small shallow trough or well built on to the upper part of the inside of the bottle. This trough is for the ink—the bottle itself has been demoted into a mere storehouse. To fill the trough you tip the full bottle, thus getting the contents over anything receptive to ink. The trough full, you now unscrew the ink-drenched lip and dip your pen into the well. As it is shallow you bang your point against the bottom. A good penpoint will survive about fifty such bangs. Three new pens to one bottle of ink is par for the course. The ink itself, by the way, is excellent.

At one time a man could ask for razor blades and get them. This is becoming increasingly difficult. My favorite blades—splendid, keen chaps—no longer come loose in a small packet. They are nested in a slotted receptacle in such a manner that if you exert just the right amount of thumb pressure on the top blade you can slide it out of the slot. The occasions when I have done this are noted in my diary. I might add that the old three-piece razor will soon be one with the American buffalo. Razors are now one-piece. They boast an ingenious system of screws and movable clamps which succeed in making the razor uncleanable, the blade loose, and the balance in the hand an uncertain quantity.

Books used to come wrapped in a piece of paper tied up with a piece of cord. In no time you could be reading the book. Today they arrive in cardboard iron maidens, suitable to the transportation of safes or pianos, without any visible weak point. Or they come swaddled in thick bags stapled at one end. The ingenious company that manufactures these bags cites their virtues: they are protective, time and labor saving, economical, space saving, simple and clean. Possibly. But they are not openable. Sometimes you can undo the staples without much loss of blood, but if you make the slightest wrong move, you tear the bag. Out flies a bushel of ancient furry shredded gray paper, the perfect stand-in for mouse dirt. This distributes itself impartially over floor, walls, and your throat and nasal passages.

Admitting without argument that I belong to that oppressed majority who are all thumbs, I would suggest that the real trouble lies elsewhere. The fact is that we are becoming victims of our surplusage and—to use a nasty seven-letter word—our know-how. In the field of prepared food and drink we cannot let well enough alone; in the field of gadgets the same thing is true. Our native ingenuity is so restless that the potentialities for change lying within the gadget begin to dominate our imaginations, drowning out any sense of that perfectly proper *resistance* to change lying within every human being. The man who falls in love with the gadget has fallen out of love with his own humanity. By fooling around too much with our materials we can outsmart ourselves. Remember the fountain pen that wrote under water. Nothing fails like excess.

The car with the automatic shift is doubtless a better car. The question is whether the subnormal who can now drive an automobile is a better man. A super-speed high-way is a better highway, but its users are slightly worse humans, because super-highway travel, with no scenery, few curves, no obstacles, is so dull as to be a kind of prison in motion. Better to watch a cow from a canal-boat than the Andes from the air.

Take bread. Mass-produced bread—or rather its pallid, sectioned ghost, hardly to be distinguished from the cellophane in which the neat slices are wrapped—is doubtless more convenient to handle; but eat enough of it and you will lose one of the oldest and most precious of human talents—the taste for the staff of life.

To relieve the over-familiarity of this doubtlessly reactionary viewpoint I think I had better refer to Aristotle. Aristotle tells us: "Moral virtue . . . is a mean between two vices, the one involving excess, the other deficiency," and, as an example, he remarks, "With regard to the giving and taking of money the mean is liberality, the excess and the defect prodigality and stinginess."

Let us now set beside Aristotle's Doctrine of the Mean another doctrine, hereafter to be known as Fadiman's Law of Optimum Improvement. I am persuaded that in the realm of objects, as well as in the realm of ethics, there can be an excess of refinement as well as a defect of crudity. It is my further conviction that a proper technological society is not the one capable of endlessly improving its artifacts, but the one able to see at what point it is best, from the point of view of the whole human being (and indeed of the whole human race), to stop the improvement.

When John Montagu, fourth Earl of Sandwich, invented the comestible named after him (he once spent twenty-four hours at the gaming table living on beef sandwiches) he placed mankind in his debt, and obeyed the doctrine of the mean. When some meddler, not satisfied with this perfect contrivance, "improved" it with lettuce, tomatoes, and other vitamin-reeking horrors, he erred in the direction of excess.

The old-fashioned kitchen was defective. The modern kitchen, with its stainless-steel double sink, its freezer, its refrigerator, is a joy, the perfect mean, improvement at its optimum. Fill it with all the "labor-saving" devices, from egg-slicers to carrot-curlers, and you have an excess, a frantic inferno of machinery.

I am not urging a return to the spinning wheel. I am only suggesting that many objects, from food to machinery, are subject to an invisible and overlooked law of maximum complication and development. Nature has wisely seen to it that human beings generally stop short at seven feet. With respect to things we must assume the role of Nature.

When I think of my own odd trade of mass communication I find myself lost in admiration before the vast technical improvements of the last thirty years, and at the same time troubled by an uneasy sense that each such improvement brings, along with its concrete benefits, some less concrete losses.

When a performer shifts from the stage to the radio microphone he says good-by to certain possibilities, among them visibility and mobility. He becomes the servant of a metal neck surmounted by a metal ear. When he transfers to the television studio he regains some visibility—but his mobility is further reduced. He has now become the servant to *two* pieces of machinery. In certain ways the camera allows him to create new effects; in other ways it circumscribes him in accordance with the unchangeable laws of its own nature. There's a television gadget called a "mixer" which permits any collection of small objects to be photographed by a special camera in such a way that they seem to comprise a full-size natural background for the actor or singer. This makes many wonderful effects possible—but the performer is even further circumscribed in his movements: any deviation outside a prescribed area will blur the image. Eventually color televison will look magnificent— to the spectator. The actor, however, will be forced to wear clothes of a particular color, to be made up in a specific way, etc.

Each of these apparently petty progressive limitations places a greater and greater distance between the personality of the performer and the performance itself. Not that the performance is uninteresting, but that its interest in part depends on the efficiency of a battery of machines. Perhaps even in the field of communication, then, works some subtle limiting law of optimum improvement.

The Sermon on the Mount, produced without benefit of even the crudest studio facilities, has since its premiere constantly enjoyed a high rating. How much would have been lost, how much gained, had it been properly produced over a coast-to-coast television network, backed by full orchestra and electric organ?

LOGAN PEARSALL SMITH

(1865–1946)

Happiness

CRICKETERS on village greens, hay-makers in the evening sunshine, small boats that sail before the wind—all these create in me the illusion of Happiness, as if a land of cloudless pleasure, a piece of the old golden World, were hidden, not (as poets have fancied) in far seas or beyond inaccessible mountains, but here close at hand, if one could find it, in some undiscovered valley. Certain grassy lanes seem to lead through the copses thither; the wild pigeons talk of it behind the woods.

INDEX OF AUTHORS

INDEX OF TITLES

THIS COLLECTION might well have been called "solely for pleasure," for the reading of the familiar essay is an experience that provides something for every mood: reflective, melancholy, or humorous. Miss Parker's selections range from the ceremonious writing of Francis Bacon to the subtle humor of E. B. White.

I Was Just Thinking— is divided into four sections; they all invite samplings. Part I, "Reading, Writing and Talking," consists of pithy essays by such writers as Charles Lamb, Francis Bacon, and Christopher Morley. Part II, "Out of Doors," is as leisurely as is a perfect spring day, and the reader can take a literary excursion with such essayists as Hilaire Belloc, Henry Thoreau, and Joseph Wood Krutch. Part III, "Traveling," presents short essays—or trips— by James Thurber, Logan Pearsall Smith, and others. Part IV, "This and That," is a delightful *potpourri*, just what the title suggests.

The compiler has made her selections with discrimination and enthusiasm. It is a personal choice that has been distilled from a wide reading in this most delightful literary form.